Kenneth Lo is the fwriting and broadcas... China, in 1913, he stu... and then English Lite... He pursued a variety o... as a diplomat, a fine-ar... ...ial relations and welfare officer for Chinese seamen, a journalist, a lecturer, and a professional tennis player. He is best known, however, for his many authoritative books on Chinese cooking and eating. He has contributed articles and columns to innumerable journals and magazines, and has appeared many times on television. The Panther edition of Kenneth Lo's *The Wok Cookbook* became an international bestseller. Now in his seventies, Kenneth Lo is still extremely active and productive, and this he attributes to the fact that he follows his own advice – about cooking and eating the Chinese way.

By the same author

Chinese Cooking Encyclopaedia
Chinese Food
Chinese Vegetable and Vegetarian Cooking
Cooking the Chinese Way
Peking Cooking
Quick and Easy Chinese Cooking
Cheap Chow
Chinese Provincial Cooking
Chinese Cooking and Eating for Health
Cooking and Eating the Chinese Way
The Wok Cookbook

KENNETH LO

More Wok Cookery

PANTHER
Granada Publishing

Panther Books
Granada Publishing Ltd
8 Grafton Street, London W1X 3LA

Published by Panther Books 1985

Copyright © Kenneth Lo 1985

ISBN 0-586-06024-3

Printed and bound in Great Britain by
Collins, Glasgow

Set in Times

All rights reserved. No part of this publication may
be reproduced, stored in a retrieval system, or
transmitted, in any form, or by any means, electronic,
mechanical, photocopying, recording or otherwise,
without the prior permission of the publishers.

This book is sold subject to the conditions that it
shall not, by way of trade or otherwise, be lent,
re-sold, hired out or otherwise circulated
without the publisher's prior consent in any
form of binding or cover other than that in
which it is published and without a similar
condition including this condition being imposed
on the subsequent purchaser.

Contents

Introduction	7
The Techniques of Wok Cooking	11
Peking and North China	21
East China	65
Szechuan and West China	131
Canton and the South East	165
Index	203

Introduction

My three gastronomic tours of China in successive years have afforded me the opportunity to observe the use of the wok throughout all the main culinary regions of China. What has been interesting to me has been to observe that, cooking being what it is, such variation as there may be between one region and another is only a matter of emphasis – the emphasis in the use of certain types of flavouring materials (i.e. more garlic, vinegar and spring onions are used in the North, more pepper and chilli in the West, more pickles and vinegar in the East and more salted black beans and seafood sauces in the South). Once you have mastered the use and handling of the wok, you can then take it through the regions of China and produce dishes of strong local colour and flavour provided that you have some acquaintance with flavouring agents and ingredients. The concocting of flavour in detail is largely a personal affair – everyone must have his or her preferences; the main thing is to grasp the 'theme' in the preparation and cooking of a given dish, and this has to be in line with the tradition of that dish in a given region. Once you have grasped the 'theme', you will seldom be at a loss. All you need is to make a few experiments, and you will soon strike the right 'note' and be able to produce dishes with a ring of authenticity, as genuinely regional (if not more so) as if they had been cooked in the regions themselves.

The issue in cooking these days is seldom one of finding the right ingredients – with improved transport and availability one can find most ingredients almost anywhere. If not, they can generally be substituted. (If no substitute can be found one might as well drop the dish – after all, there are scores of other dishes of equal interest with which one can experiment). The joy of cooking lies largely in being able to carry the dishes off and present them with style. I often compare cooking with dancing; the main thing is to grasp the theme and rhythm. Once you have achieved that, you can dance almost anything; once you have gained that confidence you will have won more than half the battle and be able to waltz through the kitchen with the wok! And to waltz through the kitchen is only one step away from waltzing through China itself.

One of the purposes of this book is purely romantic – to make the reader feel that he is on a trip through China with a wok, with the same observant eye, I hope, as Robert Louis Stevenson had when he travelled through the Pyrenees with a donkey. (Except that we have much more with which to experiment than R. L. S. could have had with his donkey!) The purpose of Stevenson's travels in the nineteenth century was to get out of the smog of England and to commune with nature under the much brighter skies of the Iberian Peninsular. The purpose of our travels with the wok is to make a pilgrimage to one of the largest gastronomic areas of the world, to investigate and savour some of the creations of this distant land – dishes which we can mostly reproduce with comparative ease using a wok in our own suburban kitchens.

We shall retrace some of the steps I took during my three gastronomic tours of China and pay pilgrimage to some of the culinary establishments that I visited (both the restaurants of renown as well as the 'unknown' cafés and eating places). We shall observe at close quarters how many of the dishes are concocted and cooked. In selecting these dishes for you to try, I shall choose those which are simple to cook; which do not indulge in the use of too many exotic ingredients, nor require dubious, outlandish food materials, such as armadillos, fruit-eating fox, five

Introduction

types of snakes, or yak's meat – dishes which I did encounter during my long trips through the vast seacoast and hinterland of China.

We shall begin our pilgrimage in Peking, nowadays called Beijing, and from there we shall proceed south to Shangtung, from where the majority of the Peking chefs have come since the days of the Ming Dynasty. From Shangtung we shall go to Sian (or Xian), site of the ancient capital of China from the time of the First Emperor, in whose tomb were found the army of terracotta figures and horses which have so held the imagination of the contemporary world. From there we shall fly westwards to Chengtu and Chungking in the province of Szechuan (Sichuan). This is the most populous province in China, where the food is well known to be spicy and hot. From there we shall follow the Yangtze River downstream as it pours through the famous Yangtze Gorges into the Central Plains of China, then floods towards the Lower Reaches. In this well-watered region of East China are situated such cities as Shanghai, Soochow, Yangchow, Nanking and Hangchow. Each of these cities has its own specialities, but their foods are much less spicy and more natural in taste than in the far west. From Shanghai we shall fly over Fukien, where I was born and bred, to Canton and eventually to Hong Kong, where the taste of seafood predominates and where fruits are abundant. We shall encounter some typical southern creativeness and indulgence. But I shall write more extensively on cooking, and especially wok cooking, in these areas as we come to them in their turn.

KENNETH LO

The Techniques of Wok Cooking

CHINESE COOKING AND THE WOK

More cooking has been performed in China than anywhere else in the world, and more cooking there is performed in the wok than in any other cooking utensil. This is partly because there are very few cookery utensils in a Chinese kitchen in any case; most utensils in the Chinese kitchen have to perform several functions. The wok, which in a Western kitchen is little more than a curve-bottomed frying pan, in China often has to double as a saucepan, deep-fryer, steamer and a double-boiler (for long simmering and braising). But above all the wok is used for stir-frying, the method of cooking which accounts for more Chinese dishes than any other method of cooking.

The proliferation of Chinese dishes into their thousands has been due mainly to the cooking of one kind of food with another, and the addition of numerous flavourings (i.e. herbs, pickles, aromatizers, etc.) at different stages of the cooking. Thus the mixing and blending of ingredients and food materials has resulted in Chinese cooking advancing from the 'elemental' to the 'compound'. In Western cooking, which is largely 'elemental' since foods are seldom mixed, there is little interaction between food materials and ingredients, whereas in Chinese cooking the mixing, blending and interaction is continuous on several planes. Whenever a new element or ingredient is added the composition and therefore the character of the dish changes. There is therefore a tendency towards an evolutionary growth of Chinese dishes from the simple to the highly complex and elaborate.

The part which the wok plays in this progression is to seal the foods and ingredients together by blending them over high heat. It is the Chinese concept and practice that the strength and flavour of many ingredients (especially the strong-tasting ones (i.e. ginger, garlic, onion, chilli, etc.) can be released and become manifest only by subjecting them to a short period of cooking over high heat. This heat treatment – frying them in hot oil, for example – has the effect of unlocking their flavours. Once the flavour is released into the oil, and the oil has become impregnated with it, it can then be used to cook or coat whatever food materials require cooking or coating. In practice, ingredients are often cooked first independently of the flavouring agents, and are only blended with the latter in the last phase of cooking. By removing the principal food material (meat, fish, seafoods or vegetables) after the initial cooking, heat-control and the timing of cooking can be more easily gauged. This results in the principal food material being more able to retain its original freshness and authenticity of flavour right to the last moment, before being blended with the flavour of the sauce, flavouring ingredients or supplementary materials, often just for an instant before the food is ready to serve and bring to the table.

STIR-FRYING

To become adept at this, one should be wholly familiar with the process of stir-frying (which is probably how 90% of dishes produced in the wok are cooked). As a rule, stir-frying in the wok is done in the two stages we have indicated. First, the principal food material is cut up small (i.e. diced, or cut into slices or shreds) and then cooked either over high heat to seal the food quickly (in order to retain most of its natural juices) or over medium heat (in order to retain the softness of the food not to cause it to stiffen due to exposure to high heat and consequent rapid drying). After this initial subjection to heat, the principal material is pushed to one side, if the subsequent cooking is to be done in the same wok.(In a restaurant, two woks are usually used: one for frying – deep or shallow – and the other for stir-frying. The one in which the stir-frying is done is where flavouring ingredients and supplementary materials are assembled and cooked and where the sauces are concocted.) The supplementary materials and flavouring ingredients and sauces are then concocted and cooked on the side of the wok, just off centre, where the heat is highest. It is only in the final phase of cooking that the lightly cooked principal materials are brought over to finish cooking with the supplementary materials as well as the flavouring ingredients and sauces. This final action brings about a 'shot-gun marriage' between the freshness and natural flavour of the principal materials and the seasoned richness and strength of flavour of the flavouring ingredients and sauces. It is always useful to bear in mind that what quick-frying in a wok usually endeavours to do is to achieve a felicitous marriage between the fresh and the matured. This is the theme. The sauce of such a marriage, which is only a by-product, is incidental to this 'matrimony'. Sauces are used to enhance the accompanying bulk foods (rice, steamed buns or noodles) rather than the meat or other principal food materials. Indeed, because foods such as meat, poultry or fish usually release their juices rapidly when subjected to the sudden impact of heat, it is true to say that the principal food material contributes largely itself to the making of the sauce.

Because of the last-minute injection of these fresh-tasting food-juices into the sauce, there is a unique quality to Chinese sauces from stir-fried dishes when they are well cooked. It is for this reason that top Chinese chefs usually use a restraining hand when adding ingredients into the wok – they do not wish to camouflage everything with strong flavours which do not allow the fresh, natural flavours to come through, freshness being just as much a part of the quality of the sauce as the ingredients which bring about the strength and precision of flavour.

BRAISING AND STEWING

This emphasis on the freshness of flavour is often emphasized just as much in Chinese cooking with braised and stewed dishes, which can also be cooked in the wok. When meat or poultry are cooked slowly over low heat and a very rich and tender dish is being produced, very often a quantity of vegetables – such as Chinese cabbage – is submerged to cook in the stock for just a short period of time before the dish is served. This large-scale inclusion of an entirely fresh material in the cooking towards the last phase of a long-cooked dish, which is about to arrive at its full maturity, dramatically changes the quality and character of the eventual product, which would otherwise be just an ordinary stew or boiled fowl. A similar and frequently practised effect is achieved in a smaller way by sprinkling a quick-fried dish with freshly chopped spring onion, parsley, shredded cucumber or broccoli tops just before the dish is served. The aim is always to add freshness to maturity, even if sometimes only in appearance. This practice is particularly marked in the preparation of top-grade Chinese chicken or meat stock, which is used extensively in Chinese cooking and flavouring. In preparing it, after prolonged boiling or simmering, and after much skimming, a quantity of freshly minced meat or minced chicken is added to cook in the stock just for a matter of a few minutes before it too is cleared and filtered away. This undoubtedly adds a distinct freshness to the stock which is very clearly felt by any practised palate.

COOKING PROCEDURE

Thus the procedure for creating flavour in Chinese wok cooking usually takes the following stages:

1. After turning the heat on under the wok for ten seconds, add 4 to 6 tablespoonfuls of oil. After a further ten seconds, when the oil is hot, add the strong-tasting vegetables – ginger, garlic, onion, spring onion, chilli or any combination of these. After stirring these vegetables in the hot oil for ½ to 1 minute, the oil will have become impregnated with their strong flavour.

2. The second stage of the cooking involves the main food materials (meat, poultry, fish, seafood, etc.). These are stir-fried in the 'flavoured oil'. The cooking time depends largely on the quantity of food materials to be cooked. Over high heat, constantly turning and stirring the food, it will generally be ¾ to 1¼ minutes (with meat, partly depending on the thickness of the cut). The turning and stirring are to ensure that the small cut pieces of meat are not only in contact with hot oil but also with the hot metal, and that every side of the meat is evenly cooked. By this time the main food material should have arrived at a point where it is three-quarters cooked. It is then pushed to the side of the wok, away from the centre of the heat. As the oil drifts back into the well of the wok, this doubly flavoured oil (flavoured by having both the meat and the strong-tasting vegetables cooked in it) is utilized for making the 'instant sauce'. This is done generally by adding a selection of materials such as soya sauce, black or yellow bean paste, hoisin sauce, oyster sauce, shrimp sauce, tomato purée and good chicken stock and wine (in quantities of 1 to 2 tablespoonfuls each). These may be added and used singly or in combinations (usually in combinations of two to three at a time, including chicken stock). When the mixture begins to bubble and boil and starts to thicken, which usually happens in a matter of 10

to 15 seconds over high heat, the main food material is brought back to be turned and mixed with the now highly flavoured sauce. Within ½ to ¾ of a minute the dish should be ready to serve.

SUPPLEMENTARY INGREDIENTS

The above is a slightly simplified version of the step-by-step procedure of stir-fry cooking in a wok. The process is slightly varied when other types of ingredients are added to achieve a further intensification or variation of flavour. For these purposes, the three following types of food materials are usually added:

1. *Dried Foods* such as mushrooms, shrimps, olives, lily buds, bacon, salted fish, etc.
2. *Pickles*. There are three principal types of pickles used by the Chinese, which nowadays can be purchased from the majority of Chinese foodstores and supermarkets. These are: (a) *Hseuh Chai* or 'Snow Pickles', which come in dark-green stem-like strips packed in small cans. They are salty and slightly vinegary in flavour. They are usually used chopped up small to stir-fry with minced or shredded meat, or to provide a strong-tasting sauce for fish, or alternatively served as a relish for bland foods such as soft rice or boiled noodles. (b) *Doong Chai* or 'Winter Pickle', which is light-brown in colour and usually contained in earthenware jars. It can be used on meat, fish or vegetables to enhance savouriness. (c) *Ja Tsai* or 'Szechuan Hot Pickle', which is a chunky root vegetable, reddish-green in colour (the red is due to red pepper being added during the pickling process). This pickle usually comes in medium-sized cans. It is used shredded or chopped into small grains. Hot and salty (even a couple of teaspoonfuls will add measurably to the hotness of the average dish), it is

extremely useful in giving a dish or soup a pronounced strength of flavour.

3. *Soya Sauce* and other soya based ingredients or derivatives such as soya paste (which comes in cans and is called 'Yellow Bean Sauce' or 'Black Bean Sauce'), Hoisin sauce – a slightly sweet, reddish-coloured, soya-based vegetable sauce, used more in South China than in the North, and frequently used in Cantonese restaurants abroad as a substitute for 'Peking Duck Sauce' to go with duck, bean curd 'cheese', and salted black beans.

These need to be soaked for a couple of minutes before they are used, and when used in stir-frying are usually stirred and mashed with other flavouring ingredients in the hot oil in which they are being cooked. Such mixtures, which sometimes include chopped chilli pepper, inject a very pronounced salty savoury flavour to a dish, which can only be described as inimitable, with a very earthy savouriness which is appealing to the majority of human palates.

4. Other ingredients which can be added to vary the flavour of the dish which is being cooked include good strong chicken stock, sugar, wine, vinegar and sesame oil. The latter is used to add a nutty flavour and a warm smoothness to the dish. Sugar (an ingredient which is much more frequently used for Chinese savoury cooking than it is ever used in the West) seems to help to increase the implicit richness of a savoury dish. The other two ingredients, wine and vinegar, are added for their more obvious contributions.

When a Chinese cook works over the wok he has therefore at his fingertips these four categories of ingredients, which I would like to call his 'four-line whip', to apply in order to vary, adjust or strengthen the flavour which he wishes to create, on top of the original taste of the main food material being cooked as well as the 'flavoured oil' which was used to cook the food in the first place.

STEAMING

Although quick or stir-fry cooking comprises no less than 80% of Chinese cooking done in the wok, there are other forms of wok cooking which are by no means unimportant. For instance, 'Quick Reduction' cooking or 'Steaming', which can be divided into 'Quick Steaming' and 'Closed Prolonged Steaming'. The former is the steaming of foods in open receptacles in a steamer, and the latter is the cooking of foods in closed receptacles in the steamer for a longer period of time, which results in the food being cooked to exceptional tenderness. (See my earlier book *The Wok CookBook*, also available in Panther Books.)

DEEP-FRYING

The wok is of course also used for deep-frying, a process which requires no introduction, but deep-frying is used in China only as the concluding phase of multi-stage cooking, which may involve parboiling, stir-frying, and steaming and roasting. In such cases, deep-frying is intended only to crisp the food just before serving. Alternatively, deep-frying is used to give the food what we call in China 'a turn in the oil', which is not serious frying as the food is submerged and turned in the hot oil for a matter of between only a few seconds to just under a minute. This process is often used initially to prepare the food for later quick or stir-frying with other food materials (for example, French beans are often given a 'turn in the oil' for a minute before they are stir-fried together with bean sprouts). The same would apply to broccoli or mangetouts.

There will be many encounters and revelations of this kind as we progress on our culinary tour of China.

Peking and North China

INTRODUCTION

The word Peking (or these days Beijing) means 'Northern Capital'. It has been the capital of China for three consecutive dynasties: Yuan (or the Mongol Dynasty), the Ming and Ching (or the Manchurian Dynasty), in addition to the Republican era as well as under the present regime the People's Republic of China.

The fact that the Manchurians and the Mongolians have between them ruled from Peking for nearly 400 years indicates that the influences of the North (both the North East and North West) as well as of the West (Sinkiang) are strong in the area. The influence of Sinkiang is largely Moslem. Moslems are not pork eaters. There is also the influence of the Silk Road which has led to sesame and other Middle Eastern ingredients creeping into Chinese cuisine. Mongolia and Manchuria are both cattle-breeding countries, and they are on the doorstep of Peking. Hence northern cooking is heavy with meat and fat (to keep people warm in the cold winters) and quite unlike that of the Yangtze regions which rely more on vegetables and fresh-water products and that of the sea-coast provinces of the South East which abound in fish, fruits and seafoods. But Peking has grown enormously during the past few decades. Acting as the capital under the People's Republic, as well as under previous Republican régimes, it has become the culinary mecca of the North. During my undergraduate days at the university there in the 1930s, Peking had a population of no more than two million. It now has a population of more than seven million. Even the famous Maxim's Restaurant of Paris, under the auspices of Pierre Cardin, has opened a branch in the Peking of today.

There are several restaurants in Peking which specialize in Peking Duck and each one of them could cook and serve more than a thousand ducks a day! Catering in China is conducted on an immense scale. It is nothing for a restaurant to seat a thousand diners – even in provincial cities – and serve several thousand covers a day. China is probably the one exception amongst the People's Republics of the world in the fact that at meal-times almost every seat in every restaurant is taken. I discovered this to my cost when I took a group of twenty well-to-do Europeans to a restaurant for a typical Cantonese breakfast one morning at 6.45 A.M., on one of our gastronomic tours. We found that every seat in the 600-seater restaurant (the Tai Ping Guan) was taken and we had to wait for some tables to be cleared for us as priority customers.

One's first impression of Peking, if one arrives in the spring, summer or autumn, is that it is an oasis compared with the sheer aridness of the steppes of Central Asia. Peking, like London, has many parks and stately buildings. The land is thickly studded with ancient trees and the boulevards and canals are all lined with trees. In most seasons the Western Hills, just beyond the western suburbs, are green with foliage, although these days because of intensive industrialization, belching chimneys are becoming an integral part of the landscape. Visually, Peking is impressive and welcoming; the air is crisp and both the sunlight by day and the moonlight by night are clear and bright. One is inclined to bask in sunshine in autumn and winter and to lie in bed to watch the moon in the spring, more so than in many other parts of the world.

But what of the smell and taste of food in the City? For these will be the sensations which one would be testing and seeking on a gastronomic tour.

Peking and North China

I think, as a Southerner, my first impression when I went North to Peking, was that the City reeked of frying garlic, lamb and leeks. It still smells much the same after fifty years! During the winter there is the added smell of chestnuts roasting in the streets. To my youthful palate, the strongest taste in the dishes I first tried was that of coriander. Coriander and all the other strong-tasting vegetables, such as onion, spring onion, garlic and ginger, are all much more heavily used in cooking in the North than in the South. It is no wonder that we from the South thought the Northerners coarse. (Quite recently I witnessed the wife of a Northern restaurateur chewing up and eating a plateful of unaccompanied cloves of garlic.) It is true that lamb and mutton are a feature of Peking food and it may be – to the Chinese at least – that such gamey and strong-tasting meat calls for some interaction with strong-tasting vegetables to arrive at an equilibrium in taste and flavour. Perhaps it is because of the cold climate (during the long winter the ground can remain frozen until March) that the Northern Chinese, like the Eskimos, are inclined to use quantities of fat in their cooking.

'Soya paste' (ground salted soya beans, often marketed in cans under the brand name 'Yellow Bean Sauce' or 'Black Bean Sauce') is heavily used in the region. Soya paste is a salty ingredient and when used in conjunction with soya sauce, which is also salty, one or the other has to be used sparingly. When a stir-fried dish is coated or finished with soya paste, it is said in local jargon to be soya paste-'exploded' on account of its being finished off in sizzling paste over high heat. It is one of the favourite ways of cooking diced or shredded meats in the North. In finishing a dish by 'exploding' in soya paste, the taste of the latter is often varied by adding a small amount of sugar, ginger or ginger-water and wine into the mix. The final flavour arrived at is very distinctive of the North.

The 'Sweet and Sour Sauce' of the North is crude by Southern standards. It consists of no more than a mixture of sugar and vinegar with a small amount of soya sauce and water added, thickened with blended cornflour. Yet this is the prevalent sauce of the region, still commonly applied to fish as in the famous Northern dish 'Yellow River Carp'.

Apart from their use in several stir-fried dishes, the pronounced flavour of strong-tasting vegetables such as garlic, ginger, spring onion, chilli, and mustard are most apparent in 'dipping sauces', used for dipping plain-cooked meats which have been poached, steamed or slow-simmered without any seasonings or flavouring ingredients. The aim here is for the meats to retain their natural flavours almost until the very point when the meat is introduced into the mouth, when they are enhanced by the strength of flavour of the dipping sauces. The same sauces are applied to stuffed dumplings and buns, another favourite food of the North, which are also cooked by steaming and poaching.

In the winter, Peking and North China are flooded with Chinese cabbages, grown in such profusion that they are often stored by piling them up on flat ground or against the walls along the sides of streets. Although often covered by layers of dust, when rinsed and washed they can appear almost pristine and jade-like in purity. They can be delectable when simply cooked in stock, when they are called 'white cooked', or with soya sauce 'red cooked' (see page 51), or when red colouring or tomato sauce is added, 'coral cabbage'. They are usually simply flavoured by adding a pinch of dried shrimp when braising. They are often also used to supplement long-cooked poultry or meat dishes in the last stage of cooking; they add a measure of sweetness and freshness to dishes which would otherwise be simply rich.

Large prawns are another item which appear frequently

Peking and North China

on tables in North China in the winter. There is usually a good crop of them coming in at this time of year from the Gulf of Chilli. As often as not they are cooked with their shells on – in consuming crustaceans we Chinese enjoy sucking the juice and sauces out of the shells as much as digging out and eating the meat.

Another feature of Peking in the winter is the 'Mongolian Hot Pot', usually cooked on the table. If you have an electrically heated wok – which are marketed nowadays by a number of manufacturers – this can be used very well instead. The 'Mongolian Hot Pot' is easy to prepare and provides diners not only with a very warming sight but also a lot of fun in its preparation. Thinly slice about 20 platefuls of lamb. Cut up 2–3 tablespoons of spring onion and prepare 2–3 slices of fresh root ginger. Put the ingredients into boiling water or stock. Boil for 2–3 minutes. Take out the lamb and eat it. The stock will have a very fresh, light flavour. Add Chinese cabbage and noodles to the stock and cook for 5–6 minutes. The resulting liquid is drunk as a soup. If you go to the famous Hot Pot Restaurant, called Tung Lai Sung, adjacent to the Tung Fen Market, you would be served first with lamb kebab before the hot pot is brought to the table. When consumed, these barbecued lamb pieces are dipped into the same dipping sauces as the lamb cooked in the hot pot.

These are some of the features of Peking during the long winter months. When spring finally comes, its arrival is marked by a feast of Spring Rolls. These Spring Rolls are made and rolled by the diners themselves, and are not fried. The principal ingredient used for stuffing the rolls is a vegetable called 'Jui Tsai', a cross between a leek and an onion. Bean sprouts and shredded meats, which are stir-fried, are invariably used to vary and enrich the contents, helping to make the feasts enjoyable occasions.

One thing that strikes the Southerner visiting the North for the first time is the quantity of pasta cooked and eaten. In the South we eat pasta (noodles, buns, dumplings, hot cakes) as snacks, but in the North they regard it as the basis of whole meals. Hence the noodles here are thicker, more like spaghetti, and eaten in larger bowls. Steamed or poached dumplings are often consumed by the dozen as staple foods. Families will sit down with grandparents, parents and children and make hundreds of them at a time. Some of the buns are without any stuffing and can be enjoyed only by dipping them into rich flavoursome gravies. Sesame-studded hotcakes are always very satisfying, and delectable when consumed with soya meats, whether hot or cold.

Noodles are particularly sumptuous when freshly hand-drawn – an almost miraculous process which northerners still practise and which takes months or years to perfect. It entails drawing a lump of well-thumped and kneaded dough into many hundreds of regular-sized spaghetti-like threads, all in a matter of minutes. These freshly made noodles normally take only four minutes to cook in simmering water. When drained they can be used in a great many ways. A favourite method is to prepare a meat sauce with minced meat and pour it over a plateful of noodles as the Italians do with their Spaghetti Bolognese, although in northern Chinese cooking the sauce is flavoured with soya paste and minced or chopped dried mushrooms, with pieces of finely shredded cucumber and spring onions for the diners to stir and toss in themselves. Although this is regarded as a rough and ready dish, it is very satisfying to eat.

Another favourite way of serving noodles is to cook them briefly in the rich broth of long-cooked meats, such as mutton or pork. When such meats have been long-simmered for 4 to 5 hours, a very rich and flavoursome broth is produced. The broth is then reconstituted and

Peking and North China

freshened up by adding some raw vegetables which are cooked in it briefly; the flavour can also be somewhat varied by the addition of a small quantity of dried mushrooms, smoked ham, bamboo shoots, etc. In the last phase of the preparation parboiled noodles are added to the stock and cooked for another 3 to 4 minutes. The dish is usually served individually in small heated casseroles, with a sprinkling of coriander leaves on top and a few chunks of very tender long-cooked meats as an accompaniment to be dipped in strong-tasting dipping sauces. Such a combination of foods makes for a satisfying and complete meal which is at the same time warm, easily digestible and healthy.

On the whole Northern Chinese cooking is less elaborate and complicated than Southern Chinese cooking although the dishes produced are equally satisfying. We shall be going through a selection of these dishes which can be prepared in the wok. When trying them out the reader should remember that most stir-fried dishes cooked in the wok are designed to be served with rice or plain-cooked noodles, plus a vegetable dish. This is because quick stir-fried dishes are seldom heavy, but they are usually rich in sauce and flavour, and are much more digestible this way. When there are more than two people dining together one should endeavour to prepare at least two savoury stir-fried dishes, if possible of contrasting materials, perhaps using different methods of cooking.

In preparing a Chinese meal it is often advantageous to cook with two woks at the same time; one for steaming and braising, and the other for stir-frying, or shallow or deep-frying. When more than one wok is in use, several dishes can easily be prepared at the same time, and the total time expended in preparing a meal is very much reduced.

SOUPS

Hot and Sour Soup *(for 4 people)*

I have often called this soup Chinese 'Junk Soup' as it can be made from almost any assortment of ingredients so long as you have a good savoury stock, a piece of bean curd and an egg. It is quick to prepare and can be cooked in one wok.

  3–4 slices root-ginger
  1 tbs Chinese 'Snow Pickles' or green mustard pickle or gherkin
  3 stalks spring onion
  4–5 large or medium-sized Chinese dried mushrooms
  1½ tbs Chinese dried shrimps
  50–75 g (2–3 oz) cooked chicken meat, pork or leftover roast beef or lamb
  1–2 cakes bean curd
  2½ tbs soya sauce
  1½ tbs cornflour (blended in 4 tbs cold water)
  4 tbs vinegar
  ¼ tsp black pepper
  1 egg lightly beaten
  1 litre (1¾ pints) good stock
  1 chicken stock cube
  1 tsp salt
  1 tsp sesame oil

Preparation

Finely chop the ginger and the pickle. Cut the spring onions into 12 mm (½ in) sections, keeping the white and green parts separate. Soak the dried mushrooms in 300 ml (½ pt) of hot water for 30 mins. Drain but reserve the water. Discard stalks and shred the caps. Soak the dried shrimps in 150 ml (¼ pt) of boiling water for 15 mins. Discard the water. Shred the meat. Cut the bean curd into

20–24 pieces. Blend the soya sauce, cornflour, water, vinegar and black pepper to a smooth paste. Lightly beat the egg.

Cooking
Heat 150 ml (¼ pint) water in the wok. When it boils add the ginger, pickle, white of onion, dried mushrooms and dried shrimps. Simmer vigorously for 5 minutes. Pour in the stock, add mushroom water and shredded meat. Crumble in stock cube and add salt. Simmer gently for 5 minutes. Add the bean curd and when the soup returns to the boil pour in the soya, cornflour, pepper and vinegar mixture, stirring all the time. The soup should now thicken. Pour the beaten egg in a thin stream, along the prongs of a fork and trail it evenly over the surface of the soup. When the egg sets, in about ½ min, sprinkle the soup with the green part of the spring onion and a little sesame oil.

Serving
This is a warm substantial soup, which can be served in bowls or soup plates. If you add another 50–75 g (2–3 oz) of shredded meat, an additional 2 cakes of bean curd and some chopped spring greens or 50–75 g (2–3 oz) broccoli, the soup will constitute a meal on its own.

Sliced Fish Pepperpot Soup *(for 4 people)*

225–350 g (½–¾ lb) white fish (plaice, sole, cod, turbot etc)
2 tsp salt
1½ tbs cornflour
1 egg white
1 litre (1¾ pints) good stock
3 slices root-ginger
25 g (1 oz) finely chopped 'Szechuan Pickle' (optional)

3 stalks spring onion
1 chicken stock cube
2 tbs light soya sauce
3 tbs vinegar
¼ tsp pepper
1 tsp sesame oil

Preparation
Cut the fish into 2.5 × 5 cm (1 × 2 in) slices. Rub with 2 tsp salt, the cornflour and egg white. Blanch in boiling water for 1 min, drain and put aside. Clean and cut the spring onion into 2.5 cm (1 in) pieces, separating out the green and white parts. Finely chop the pickle.

Cooking
Heat stock in a wok. When it boils add the ginger, pickle, the white part of the spring onion, the remainder of the salt, the stock cube and the soya sauce. Let it boil again and then allow it to simmer gently for 2 mins. Now add the vinegar, pepper and the blanched slices of fish. When it returns to the boil allow it to simmer for another min. Sprinkle with the green parts of the spring onion and the sesame oil.

Serving
Serve in a large bowl or tureen so the diners can help themselves. This is a light soup and in the context of a Chinese meal should be eaten throughout the meal rather than all in one go at the start of the meal.

Sliced Lamb Pepperpot Soup with Sliced Cucumber *(for 4–5 people)*

The aromatic qualities of the spring onion and sesame oil coupled with the spicy sharpness of the pepper and vinegar in this soup are reminiscent of winter in Beijing.

Peking and North China

125–150 g (4–5 oz) piece of leg of lamb (or any other cut of lamb)
2 tsp salt, ¼ tsp pepper
1½ tbs cornflour
1 egg white
7.5 cm (3 in) piece medium size cucumber
1.1 litres (2 pints) good stock
3 slices root ginger
25 g (1 oz) Ja Tsai Pickles (optional)
3 stalks spring onion
1 chicken stock cube
2 tbs light soya sauce
3 tbs vinegar
½ tsp sesame oil

Preparation, Cooking and Serving

Cut the meat up and prepare as the fish in the previous recipe. Cut the cucumber into very thin slices and then into matchstick shreds. Repeat the previous recipe, adding the cucumber when the lamb is returned to the wok. When serving, sprinkle the sesame oil over the soup with the green parts of the spring onions.

Sliced Beef and Tomato Soup *(for 4–5 people)*

Because of the profusion of tomatoes in Beijing in the summer, this soup is as reminiscent of the summer there as the previous dish recalls winter in the city.

125–150 g (4–5 oz) fillet of beef
1 tsp salt
1 tbs dark soya sauce
1½ tbs cornflour
1 egg white
4–5 firm, medium-sized tomatoes
2 stalks spring onion

25 g (1 oz) Ja Tsai Pickles (optional)
1.1 litres (2 pints) good stock
2 slices root-ginger
1 chicken stock cube
2 tbs light soya sauce
1 tsp sesame oil

Preparation
Cut the beef into very thin slices, about 2.5 × 5 cm (1 × 2 in). Rub evenly and thoroughly with salt, dark soya sauce, cornflour and egg white. Leave to marinade for 30 mins. Slice 2 of the tomatoes thinly and cut the rest into 6 wedges each. Cut the spring onions into 6 mm (¼ in) pieces. Chop and mince the pickle.

Cooking
Heat the stock in the wok. Add ginger, pickle, crumbled stock cube and light soya sauce. When it boils, add the tomato pieces and allow them to simmer for 3–4 mins. Add the marinated beef. Continue to simmer for 2–3 mins. Sprinkle with spring onion and sesame oil and cook for another ½ min.

Serving
This is a comparatively light soup and in China is normally taken throughout the meal and is, therefore, best served in a large soup tureen so that the diners can help themselves.

Sliced Duck Liver Soup with Chinese Cabbage *(for 4–5 people)*

This is a soup which is often served in the Peking Duck Restaurant in Beijing, when 'Duck Carcass' soup is not served, in order to use up all the bits and pieces of the duck. When over a thousand ducks are cooked every day in a restaurant, there are usually a great many bits and pieces of duck to be used up. The addition of chopped fresh coriander gives the soup a very pronounced North Chinese flavour.

It is best to prepare this soup using two woks as the two parts of the soup are initially cooked separately and are only combined for a final momentary cooking just before serving.

Soup
150–175 g (5–6 oz) duck liver
½ tsp salt
1 tbs dark soya sauce
1½ tbs spring onions
1½ tbs fresh coriander
900 ml–1.1 litres (1½–2 pt) good stock
3 slices root-ginger
1 chicken stock cube
1½ tbs vinegar
1 tbs light soya sauce
3 tbs dry sherry

Sauce
6 medium-sized Chinese dried mushrooms
1 tbs dried shrimps
1 tbs vegetable oil
1 tbs chicken fat
1 medium-sized onion
1 tbs brown bean paste
2 tbs cornflour (blended in 5 tbs cold water)

Preparation
Cut the duck liver into 1 × 4 cm (½ × 1½ in) thin slices. Rub and marinate with salt, pepper and dark soya sauce. Leave to season for 1 hour. Soak the dried mushrooms and the dried shrimps in 600 ml (1 pint) boiling water for 20 mins. Drain and reserve the water. Discard the

mushroom stems and shred the caps. Chop the spring onion and the fresh coriander.

Cooking and Serving
Prepare the sauce by heating the oil and fat in a small wok. When hot add the onion, shrimps and mushrooms. Stir them together over medium heat for 1½ mins. Add the bean paste and bring to the boil. Leave to simmer gently until the sauce has been reduced by half. Stir in the blended cornflour and cook for 1 min.

Meanwhile, heat the stock in another larger wok. Add the ginger, crumbled stock cube, vinegar, light soya sauce and sherry. When it comes to the boil add the pieces of duck liver. Leave to simmer for 2 minutes. Finally, pour the contents of the smaller wok (the sauce) into the soup. Stir them together over a high heat. When it begins to boil vigorously, sprinkle with the spring onion and fresh coriander.

Duck Liver and Chinese White Cabbage Soup *(for 4–5 people)*

This is a completely different version of Duck Liver Soup which is prepared in quite a different way, but also uses two woks.

about 700 g (1½ lb) Chinese cabbage
150–175 g (5–6 oz) duck liver
2 tbs dark soya sauce
salt and pepper (to taste)
2 tbs dried shrimps
2 stalks spring onion
900 ml (1½ pints) good stock
2 slices root-ginger
1 chicken stock cube
2 tbs vegetable oil

1 tsp sesame oil
3 tbs sherry

Preparation
Clean and cut the cabbage into 4 cm (1½ in) slices. Cut the duck liver into 1 × 4 cm (½ × 1½ in) slices and marinade as in the previous recipe. Soak the dried shrimps in 150 ml (¼ pint) of boiling water for 15 mins. Drain and discard water. Finely mince the spring onion.

Cooking
Heat the stock in a wok. When it boils add the cabbage, dried shrimps, ginger, crumbled stock cube and salt and pepper to taste. Simmer gently for 15 mins. Whilst the cabbage is cooking, heat the vegetable and sesame oil in a smaller wok. When it is hot, add the spring onion, the sliced marinated liver, soya sauce and the sherry. Stir over a medium heat for 2½ mins.

Serving
Pour the contents of the wok containing the cabbage shrimp soup into a large soup bowl or tureen. Top with the duck liver mixture. This is what in China we often call a 'semi-soup' dish which is normally eaten with all the other dishes on the table and accompanies rice. The interest lies in the combination of a savoury item, such as liver, with the comparative purity of the cabbage soup. This goes down extremely well with quantities of rice.

Minced Chicken Soup with Croûtons and Ham *(for 4 people)*

This is a very popular winter soup in North China, it can also be made with white flaked fish, instead of chicken. This soup also needs to be cooked in two woks.

Soup
150–175 g (5–6 oz) cooked chicken meat
50 g (2 oz) ham
1 egg white
900 ml (1½ pints) good stock
1½ chicken stock cubes
2 slices finely chopped root-ginger
3 tbs dry sherry
2 tbs cornflour (blended with 6 tbs cold water)
1 tsp salt and pepper (to taste)

Croûtons
1½ slices of bread
2 tbs fresh coriander
2 tbs spring onion
1 tbs vegetable oil (for shallow frying)

Preparation
Coarsely chop the chicken and ham. Beat the egg white lightly. Remove crust from the bread and cut into small cubes. Finely chop the spring onions and the coriander.

Cooking
Heat the stock in a wok. When it starts to boil add the chopped chicken and ham, crumbled stock cubes and ginger. Simmer for 5–6 mins. Add half the sherry and the blended cornflour. Season with salt and pepper. Cook and stir for 1 min. Slowly stir in the egg white in a thin stream. Sprinkle the top of the soup with the remaining sherry.

Meanwhile, heat the oil in a smaller wok. When it is very hot add the bread cubes and fry them over a high heat until crisp and brown, about 1–1½ mins. Remove and drain.

Serving
Place the croûtons, chopped spring onion and coriander at the bottom of a well-heated bowl and bring to the table. Pour the hot soup over this and serve.

Minced or Flaked Fish Soup with Ham and Croûtons *(for 4 people)*

Repeat the previous recipe using 150–175 g (5–6 oz) white fish. Parboil the fillet of any white fish for 4–5 mins. Drain and mince coarsely. Use the minced fish in precisely the same manner as the minced chicken in the previous recipe.

QUICK STIR-FRIED SAVOURY DISHES

Quick-fried Diced Chicken Cubes in Yellow Bean Paste Sauce *(for 4 people)*

225–350 g (½–¾ lb) chicken breast meat
1½ tbs cornflour
1 egg white
4½ tbs vegetable oil

Sauce
2½ tbs ginger-water (blended in 2 tsp cornflour)
2 tbs yellow bean paste (available in cans)
1 tbs dark soya sauce
1 tbs sugar
2 tbs dry sherry

Preparation
Cut the chicken meat into sugar lump-sized cubes. Sprinkle and rub evenly with cornflour and wet with egg white. Prepare ginger-water by boiling 3 slices of root-ginger with 5 tbs water until the liquid is reduced by

half. Allow it to cool before blending it with the cornflour.

Cooking
Heat the oil in a wok. When hot add the chicken cubes and stir them quickly over a high heat for 1½ mins, remove; drain and put aside.

Add the bean paste, soya sauce and sugar to the remaining oil in the wok. Pour in the sherry and the blended ginger-water. Stir until the mixture thickens and is creamy and bubbling. Return the fried chicken to the wok. Over a high heat, turn it and mix it with the sauce, stirring for about 1¼ mins. The dish is now ready to serve.

Serving
Serve on a well-heated serving dish. This is a delicious dish, very typical of Beijing, to be eaten with rice and plain-cooked vegetables.

Note
The above dish is often cooked with nuts added (cashew nuts, peanuts, almonds etc). First stir-fry 50–75 g (2–3 oz) nuts in 2 tbs of oil for 1–1½ mins and then remove them. Add a further 2½ tbs oil to the wok and add the diced chicken cubes. Proceed as for the above recipe, adding the nuts with the chicken at the end of the recipe.

Some people prefer the dish with the addition of nuts as their flavour and crispy texture make a good contrast to rice.

Quick-fried Three Types of Diced Meat Cubes in Bean Paste Sauce *(for 4–5 people with 1 or 2 other dishes)*

Because of the contrasting textures and flavours of the three meats used in this dish, it is often served as a dish to be nibbled at when the Chinese are sipping wine in 'tea shops' and surburban restaurants.

150–175 g (5–6 oz) fillet of pork
100 g (¼ lb) pork liver
100 g (¼ lb) pork kidney
1½ tbs salt
2 tbs cornflour
5¾ tbs vegetable oil

Sauce
4 tbs ginger-water (blended with 1 tbs cornflour)
2½ tbs bean paste sauce
1 tbs sugar
1½ tbs dark soya sauce
2 tbs dry sherry

Preparation
Dice the pork, liver and kidney into small sugar lump-sized cubes. Sprinkle and rub them evenly with salt, cornflour and ¾ tbs of vegetable oil.

Prepare the ginger-water by boiling 3 slices of ginger in 6 tbs of water until the liquid has reduced by half. Allow the mixture to cool before blending with cornflour.

Cooking
Heat 3 tbs of oil in a wok. When hot add the pork cubes and fry them quickly. Turn and stir quickly over a high heat for 1½ mins; remove and put aside. Add another 2 tbs of oil to the wok. When hot put in the liver and kidney and stir-fry quickly over a high heat for 1 min. Remove and set aside to drain.

Add the bean paste, sugar and soya sauce to the remainder of the oil in the wok. Heat and stir quickly for 10–15 secs. Pour in the blended cornflour and ginger-water and cook, stirring quickly until the sauce is well blended and bubbling. Return the diced pork, liver and kidney cubes to the wok. Stir and cook quickly over a high heat for about 1 min so that they are thoroughly coated in the sauce. Serve.

Serving
Serve on a well-heated dish and accompany with rice and plain-cooked vegetables.

Quick-fried Diced Chicken with Gammon and Cucumber Cubes (*for 4–5 people with 1 or 2 other dishes*)

225 g (½ lb) breast of chicken
100 g (¼ lb) gammon
1½ tsp salt
pepper (to taste)
3½ tbs oil
¾ tbs cornflour
15 cm (6 in) piece medium-sized cucumber
2 stalks spring onion
2–3 cloves garlic
3 tbs good stock
1½ tbs dry sherry
1 tbs light soya sauce

Preparation
Cut the chicken and gammon into small sugar lump-sized cubes. Sprinkle and rub the chicken cubes with salt, pepper, ½ tbs oil and cornflour. Cut the cucumber into similar-sized cubes and finely chop the spring onions. Crush the garlic and chop it coarsely.

Cooking
Heat oil in a wok. When hot, add chicken and gammon and stir-fry over high heat for 1½ mins. Add the cucumbers, stock, sherry, garlic and soya sauce. Continue to cook and turn over a high heat for 2 mins.

Serving
Serve on a well-heated serving dish and eat as an accompaniment to rice, or as a nibble with wine. This is a neat, clear, light-coloured dish, which is very savoury.

Quick-fried Five Shredded Ingredients *(for 4–5 people with 1 or 2 other dishes)*

100 g (¼ lb) lean pork
75 g (3 oz) ham or gammon
salt and pepper (to taste)
4 tbs vegetable oil
75–100 g (3–4 oz) bamboo shoots
1 medium-sized young carrot
2 stalks spring onion
6 medium-sized Chinese dried mushrooms
2 slices root-ginger
2 cloves garlic
3 tbs good stock
1½ tbs light soya sauce
½ chicken stock cube
1½ tbs dry sherry
1 tsp sesame oil

Preparation
Cut the pork and gammon into large matchstick-sized shreds. Rub pork with salt, pepper and 1 tsp of oil. Cut the bamboo shoots and carrots into similar shreds and the spring onion into 5 cm (2 in) pieces. Soak the mushrooms for 30 mins. Drain and reserve the liquid. Discard the mushroom stalks and cut the caps into thin shreds.

Cooking
Heat the remaining oil in a wok. When hot add the pork and gammon and turn and stir them around a few times. Add bamboo shoots, mushrooms, carrots, ginger and

continue to stir over a high heat for 2 mins. Add the spring onions, garlic, mushroom liquid, stock, soya sauce, and the crumbled stock cube. Turn a few times and leave to cook over a reduced heat for another 2 mins. Sprinkle sherry and sesame oil in. Raise the heat, turn and stir quickly a few times. Serve.

Serving
Like the previous dish, this is also meant to be eaten with rice. The contrast of textures of its ingredients makes this dish especially appealing when eaten with rice.

Stir-fried Pork, Dried Shrimps and Vegetables with Pea-starch Transparent Noodles *(for 4–5 people)*

Cook this dish with the same ingredients and in the same way as the previous one but augment it by adding 75–100 g (3–4 oz) of pea-starch noodles soaked in water for 15 mins and cut into 7.5 cm (3 in) lengths. Add the noodles to the wok at the same time as the spring onions and stock. Also increase the stock to 7 tbs and the soya sauce to 5½ tbs.

In spite of this small increase, the dish should now help feed an extra mouth. If one or two additional guests arrive unexpectedly in China, and there are already several savoury dishes on the table, all that is needed is an extra bowl or two of rice.

Stir-fried Shredded Pork with Leeks and Transparent Noodles *(for 4–5 people)*

Unlike the previous dish, this one is meant to be cooked as a 'semi-soup dish'.

1½ tbs dried shrimps
5 medium-sized Chinese dried mushrooms
3 stalks young leeks
75–100 g (3–4 oz) transparent pea-starch noodles
3 tbs vegetable oil
1 chicken stock cube
½ tsp salt and pepper (to taste)
75–100 g (3–4 oz) pork
300–450 ml (½–¾ pint) good stock
1½ tbs light soya sauce
2 tbs sherry
1 tsp sesame oil

Preparation
Soak the shrimps and mushrooms in 150 ml (¼ pint) boiling water for 20 mins. Drain and reserve the liquid. Discard the mushroom stems and shred the caps. Wash the leeks thoroughly and cut into 7.5 cm (3 in) lengths then cut each piece lengthwise into quarters. Soak the noodles in warm water for 10 mins and cut into 7.5 cm (3 in) lengths in the water and drain.

Cooking
Heat the oil in a wok. When hot, add the pork, mushrooms and dried shrimps and season to taste with salt and pepper. Stir-fry for 2 mins, over a medium heat. Add the leeks and pour in the mushroom/shrimp water. Sprinkle in the crumbled stock cube and turn the heat up high. When the mixture comes to the boil, turn and stir the ingredients together for 1½ mins. Pour in the stock and add the noodles. When it returns to the boil, sprinkle in the soya sauce and sherry. Leave to cook for 4–5 mins, stirring now and again. Just before serving, sprinkle with sesame oil.

White-cooked Sliced Pork *(for 4–5 people)*

1.1 kg (2½ lb) belly pork
4 slices root-ginger
2 tsp salt

Dipping Sauce
3 cloves garlic
3 stalks spring onion
4 tbs dark soya sauce
3 tbs vinegar
1½ tbs chilli sauce
1 tbs sherry
1 tsp sesame oil

Preparation
Cut pork through the skin into 4 pieces. Coarsely chop the garlic and spring onions.

Cooking
Bring 1.4 litres (2½ pints) of water to the boil in a wok. Add ginger, salt and the pork pieces. Bring back to the boil. Reduce the heat and let the pork simmer gently for 45 mins. Drain the meat. Cut the pork again through the skin into 7.5 × 10 cm (3 × 4 in) thin slices, each one of these should have some lean, fat and skin which should be almost jelly-like.

Prepare the dipping sauce by mixing the chopped garlic and spring onions with the soya sauce, vinegar, chilli sauce, sherry and sesame oil.

Serving
Arrange the slices of pork on a serving dish to give a tile-like effect. Dip into the sauce and then eat.

Stir-fried and Braised Chinese Spare-ribs *(for 4–5 people)*

In China, spare-ribs are cut short 4–5 cm (1½–2 in) which makes it easier to stir-fry them. In the West they are usually eaten long.

1.6 kg (3½ lbs) spare-ribs
4½ tbs vegetable oil
4 tbs light soya sauce
6 slices root-ginger
2 stalks spring onion
700 ml (1¼ pints) good stock
1½ tbs sugar
4 tbs yellow bean paste sauce
2 tbs dark soya sauce
3 tbs dry sherry
1½ tbs cornflour (blended in 6 tbs cold water)
pepper (to taste)

Preparation
Cut spare-ribs into individual ribs and parboil for 4–5 mins. Chop with a cleaver into 5 cm (2 in) lengths. Rub in ½ tbs of oil and the light soya sauce. Shred the ginger and finely chop the spring onions.

Cooking
Heat the remaining oil in a wok. When hot add the ginger and the spare-ribs. Stir-fry over a high heat for 3–4 mins. Add stock, sugar, bean paste sauce and dark soya sauce. Return to the boil and turn the ribs over a few times. Place a lid over the wok and leave to cook over a medium heat for 30 mins, turning the ribs every 10 mins. Then cook for a further 10–12 mins without the lid, if necessary over high heat, until the liquid in the wok is almost dry. Add the sherry and the blended cornflour. Raise the heat to high and stir for 2 mins. Season with pepper.

Serving
Transfer the ribs and sauce into a well-heated, deep-sided serving dish. Sprinkle with spring onion and serve.

Quick-fried Beef Ribbons with Sliced Onions (*for 5 people with 1 or 2 other dishes*)

If you have some good beef this is a very quick dish to cook which can give as much pleasure and satisfaction as any of the foregoing dishes but unlike them it takes only 5–6 mins to make.

    450–550 g (1–1¼ lb) good beef steak
    1 tsp salt
    pepper (to taste)
    1½ tbs cornflour
    ½ egg white
    5 tbs vegetable oil
    2 large onions
    2 tbs dark soya sauce
    1 tbs yellow bean paste
    2 tbs good stock
    2 tbs dry sherry
    ¾ tbs sugar

Preparation
Cut beef into 6 mm (¼ in) wide and 5 cm (2 in) long very thin ribbons. Sprinkle and rub evenly with salt, pepper, cornflour and wet with the egg white. Cut the onions into very thin slices.

Cooking
Heat 4 tbs of oil in a wok. When hot add the beef and turn and stir vigorously over a high heat for 1½ mins. Remove. Add the balance of the oil to the wok and add the sliced onions. Stir-fry them over a medium heat for 2 mins. Add

the remaining ingredients and stir them together for 2 mins. The onions will have broken down into shreds at this stage. Return the beef to the wok, stir and turn it in the sauce for 1 min.

Serving
Serve hot with rice. The distinct taste of beef smothered with onions in a sauce of sweet, salty and 'earthy' savouriness presents a combination which is highly appetizing to all palates.

Shallow-fried Onion-smothered Fish *(for 4–5 people)*

This is not an haute cuisine Chinese dish, but it is a highly-prized household dish which true-born Chinese often dream about when they are abroad.

    3 slices root-ginger (chopped coarsely)
    700–900 g (1½–2 lb) fish (whole fish, cutlets or steaks)
    1 tsp salt
    pepper (to taste)
    2 tbs cornflour
    6½ tbs vegetable oil
    4 tbs soya sauce (dark or light)
    6–8 stalks spring onion
    ¾ tbs sugar
    1½ tbs yellow bean paste
    2 tbs hoisin sauce (optional)
    4 tbs good stock
    3 tbs dry sherry

Preparation
Coarsely chop the ginger. Rub the fish evenly with salt, pepper, cornflour, ½ tbs oil and sprinkle in the ginger. Cut spring onions into 2.5 cm (1 in) lengths (keeping the white and green separate).

Cooking

Heat the remaining oil in a wok. When hot add the fish or fish pieces and cook for 2 mins on either side, basting with hot oil all the time. Remove the fish or fish pieces and put aside. Add the white parts of the spring onions and the ginger to the wok and stir quickly in the oil for 1 min. Add the green parts of the spring onions and stir them all together for ½ min. Push everything to the side of the wok. Add the remaining ingredients to the centre of the wok. Stir and mix them together over a medium heat to produce a sauce and return the fish to the wok. Turn and coat it evenly with the sauce. Push a quarter of the spring onions and ginger mixture under the fish and put the remainder on top of it. Baste a few times with the sauce. Reduce the heat to low and cook gently, covered, over a low heat for 5–6 mins. The sauce should now be reduced to about a quarter.

Serving

Serve on a well-heated deep-sided serving dish. It is doubtful whether there is a more appealing fish dish in any culinary repertoire to accompany steamed or boiled rice.

'White-braised' Chinese Cabbage with Shrimps *(for 4–6 people with 1 or 2 other dishes)*

In China a dish which is cooked without soya sauce is often called 'white cooked' or 'white braised'.

  about 900 g (2 lb) Chinese cabbage
  1 medium-sized onion
  3 tsp dried shrimps
  3 tbs vegetable oil
  1½ tsp salt
  300 ml (½ pint) good stock
  1½ chicken stock cubes

1 tbs butter
freshly ground pepper (to taste)

Preparation
Cut the cabbage into 4 cm (1½ in) slices. Thinly cut the onions. Soak the dried shrimps in hot water for 20 mins.

Cooking
Heat oil in the wok. When hot add onion and salt and stir-fry over medium heat for 1½ mins. Add the cabbage and turn it in the hot oil with the onion for 2 mins. Add the stock, dried shrimps and sprinkle with crumbled stock cube. When it comes to the boil turn the cabbage over a few times in the stock, cover and simmer for 10 mins. Stir in the butter and grind the pepper on top.

Serving
Although this is a simple dish, it is a very satisfying one when eaten with rice, meat and savoury dishes.

Red-cooked Chinese Cabbage

A dish is considered 'red-cooked' when soya sauce is used in its preparation. Repeat the previous recipe but instead of using salt, add 2½ tbs of soya sauce and 1 tbs of sugar when the stock is being added to the wok. Because of the enriching effect of the sugar, some people prefer this version to the previous one. Generally speaking, when there are many other dishes on the table which contain soya sauce the 'white-braised' version is preferred; on the other hand, when most of the dishes on the table are steamed, simmered and stir-fried without much soya sauce, the 'red-cooked' version is more likely to be served.

More Wok Cookery

Quick-fried Shredded Chicken with French Beans *(for 4–5 people with 1 or 2 other dishes)*

200–225 g (7–8 oz) breast of chicken
1 tsp salt
pepper (to taste)
2 tbs cornflour
1 egg white
225 g (½ lb) French beans
2 cloves garlic
1 tbs dried shrimps
4 tbs vegetable oil
3 tbs good stock
1½ tbs light soya sauce
2 tbs dry sherry
1 tbs tomato purée
1 tbs shrimp sauce

Preparation
Cut the chicken meat into 6.5 cm (2½ in) long matchsticks. Sprinkle and rub evenly with salt, pepper and cornflour. Wet with egg white. Top and tail the French beans and blanch in boiling water for 2 mins. Drain. Crush and chop the garlic coarsely. Soak the dried shrimps in hot water for 20 mins; drain and chop coarsely.

Cooking
Heat 3 tbs of oil in a wok. When hot add the chicken, a few pieces at a time. Separate them from one another and stir-fry quickly over a high heat for 1½ mins. Remove and drain. Add the remaining oil to the wok. Add garlic, dried shrimps and French beans. Stir-fry them in the hot oil for 2 mins. Add stock, soya sauce, sherry, tomato purée and shrimp sauce. Turn and stir them together for 2 mins over high heat. Return the chicken to the wok and cook all the ingredients together, stirring for 1½ mins.

Peking and North China

Serving
A highly savoury and colourful dish which should be eaten immediately it is cooked.

Stir-fried Bean Sprouts with Shredded Pork *(for 4–5 people with 1 or 2 other dishes)*

- 100 g (¼ lb) lean pork
- 1 tsp salt
- pepper (to taste)
- 3½ tbs vegetable oil
- 225 g (½ lb) fresh bean sprouts
- 2 stalks spring onion
- 1 tbs butter or lard
- 1 tbs light soya sauce
- 2 tbs good stock
- ½ tbs vinegar
- 1 tsp sesame oil

Preparation
Cut the pork into matchstick shreds. Rub with salt and pepper and sprinkle on ½ tbs oil. Wash the bean sprouts and drain well. Cut the spring onions into 12 mm (½ in) lengths.

Cooking
Heat the remainder of the oil in a wok. When hot add the pork and stir-fry quickly over a high heat for 1½ mins. Add butter or lard. Add the bean sprouts and stir-fry with the pork for 1½ mins. Add the soya sauce, stock and vinegar. Continue to turn and mix over a high heat for 1½ mins. Sprinkle with the chopped spring onions and sesame oil.

Serving
This is a good dish to serve to balance pure meat and fish

dishes. The crispness of the bean sprouts contrasts well with the softness of boiled rice which is eaten at the same time.

Stir-fried Spinach with Garlic and Dried Shrimps *(for 4–5 people with 1 or 2 other dishes)*

450 g (1 lb) young spinach
3 cloves garlic
1 tbs dried shrimps
3½ tbs vegetable oil
1½ tbs butter
1 tbs light soya sauce

Preparation
Remove the tougher stems of the spinach. Tear the leaves roughly into 7.5 × 5 cm (3 × 2 in) pieces. Wash and drain thoroughly. Crush and coarsely chop the garlic. Soak the dried shrimps for 30 mins in hot water. Drain and chop them.

Cooking
Heat the oil in a wok. Swivel around so that a large surface area of it is greased. Add the garlic and shrimps. Turn and stir them around a few times for about ½ min. Add the spinach and turn it in the hot oil. Stir and make sure that every leaf is greased. Add the butter and sprinkle with the soya sauce. Cook and stir for another 1½ mins.

Serving
By now this vegetable dish should be a glistening green colour. It is ideal served as a contrast to a pure meat dish and as a compliment to plain boiled rice.

Steamed Aubergine with Tomatoes and Dried Shrimps *(for 4–5 people with 1 or 2 other dishes)*

350 g (¾ lb) aubergine
350 g (¾ lb) tomatoes
1 medium-sized onion
2 cloves garlic
1½ tbs dried shrimps
3 tbs vegetable oil
75 g (3 oz) minced pork
½ tsp salt
2½ tbs soya sauce
3 tbs good stock

Preparation
Cut each aubergine into 15 wedge-shaped pieces and the tomatoes into 12 wedge-shaped pieces. Thinly slice the onion. Place the aubergine and tomato at the bottom of a deep heatproof bowl. Cover them with onion slices. Crush and chop the garlic coarsely. Soak the dried shrimps for 20 mins. Drain and chop coarsely.

Cooking
Heat oil in a wok. When hot add the garlic, dried shrimps, minced pork and salt. Stir over a high heat for 1½ mins. Add soya sauce and stock and cook, stirring, for another 1½ mins. Pour this mixture over the aubergine, tomatoes and onion in the heatproof bowl. Cover dish with foil.

Rinse and wash out the wok. Fill with 1.1 litres (2 pints) of water. Bring the water to the boil as quickly as possible and stand the heatproof bowl in the boiling water at the centre of the wok. Cover the wok and simmer for 45 mins, by which time the vegetables in the bowl should be well cooked.

Serving
Bring the heatproof bowl to the table and let the diners help themselves, spooning the dish onto their rice.

Savoury Steamed Egg-Custard with Crab Meat (*for 4–5 people with 1 or 2 other dishes*)

Although a simple dish, this is one of the prized dishes of Chinese household cooking.

    1 tbs dried shrimps
    425 ml (¾ pint) good stock
    1½ tsp salt
    1 chicken stock cube
    3 eggs
    3–4 tbs cooked crab meat
    2 tbs peas
    1 tbs chopped spring onion

Preparation
Soak the dried shrimps in hot water for 20 mins. Drain them. Heat the stock in a saucepan. Add the salt, crumbled stock cube and drained shrimps. Stir when the liquid starts to boil. Turn off the heat and leave to cool for 1 hour. Beat the eggs lightly and stir them into the stock blending them well. Shred the cooked crab meat.

Cooking
Pour the egg and stock mixture into a deep heatproof bowl. Stand the bowl, in a wok three-quarters full of boiling water. Cover the wok with a lid and keep the water boiling vigorously for 20 mins. (Note the heatproof bowl is left uncovered so that its contents is subjected to 'open steaming'.) The top of the egg custard should now be firm enough for the crab meat and peas to be placed lightly on top of the custard. Close the lid of the wok and continue

to 'open steam' for a further 5–6 mins. Sprinkle the top of the 'custard' with spring onion.

Serving
Bring the heatproof bowl to the table. A large spoon should be provided for the diners to ladle the savoury egg-custard, crab meat and peas onto the rice already in their bowls. Soya sauce can be sprinkled on the custard either before or after it has been ladled from the bowl.

Stir-fried Eggs with Onion and Tomatoes *(for 5 people)*

This is a very simple but popular household dish.

1 medium-sized onion
4–5 medium-sized tomatoes
5 eggs
½ tsp salt
good pinch of pepper
2 stalks spring onion
5 tbs vegetable oil
2 tbs dark soya sauce

Preparation
Cut the onion into very thin slices and the tomatoes into 6 wedge-shaped segments each. Beat the eggs with a fork a dozen times. Add salt and pepper and beat again a dozen times. Cut the spring onions in half lengthwise and then into 5 cm (2 in) lengths.

Cooking
Heat 2½ tbs of oil in the wok. When hot add the onion and turn it in the oil over high heat for 1½ mins. Add the tomatoes and continue to turn and stir with the onions over a medium heat for 1 min. Remove and put aside. Add the remaining oil to the wok. Lift the handle of the

wok so that the oil will grease a wide area of the surface. When the oil is hot pour in the beaten eggs and stir. When the eggs are three-quarters set turn them over. Return the tomatoes and onion to the wok and mix and turn them lightly with the eggs.

Serving
Turn the contents of the wok out on to a well-heated serving dish. Sprinkle with soya sauce and spring onions and serve.

Buddhist 'Food of the Forest for the Immortals' *(for 5–6 people with 1 or 2 other dishes)*

3 tbs 'woodears'
2–3 stalks dried lily buds
5–6 Chinese dried mushrooms
1¼ tbs bean curd 'cheese'
75 g (3 oz) chestnuts
3 sticks asparagus
75 g (3 oz) pea-starch transparent noodles
1½ cakes Chinese bean curd
2 bean curd sticks (optional)
6 tbs vegetable oil
75–100 g (3–4 oz) button mushrooms
2 tbs light soya sauce
1 tsp sesame oil
4 tbs rice wine or dry sherry
50–75 g (2–3 oz) bamboo shoots

Preparation
Cover the 'woodears' and lily buds in plenty of water and leave to soak for 20 mins. Drain. Soak the dried mushrooms in 600 ml (1 pint) of boiling water for 30 mins. Drain and reserve the liquid. Mash the bean curd 'cheese' into this mushroom water until it is a smooth consistency.

Discard the mushroom stems. Parboil the chestnuts and asparagus for 5 mins and then drain. Discard the tougher parts of the asparagus stalks. Cut the remainder slantwise into 5 cm (2 in) lengths. Soak the transparent noodles in cold water for 15 mins. Whilst still in the water cut into 8–11.5 cm (3–4 in) sections. Drain. Cut the bean curd cakes into a dozen pieces. Soak the bean curd sticks in warm water for 30 mins. Drain. Heat the oil in a small pan. When hot add the bean curd pieces and stir-fry them for 2–3 mins. Drain.

Cooking

Pour the oil from the small pan into a large wok. Add the bean curd 'cheese' and mushroom water mixture. Stir over a medium heat, for 2 mins. Add all the other ingredients, except the rice wine and sesame oil, bring to the boil and simmer, covered, for 20 mins. Sprinkle with rice wine or sherry and sesame oil.

Serving

This makes a large dish of food. It should be served in a large bowl or soup tureen and brought to the table for the diners to help themselves.

NOODLES

Vegetarian Cooked-in-the-Wok Noodles *(for 4 people)*

The previous recipe can be transformed into a light vegetarian meal for 4 people by making a few simple changes. Substitute 450 g (1 lb) of wheat-flour noodles (or spaghetti) for the pea-starch noodles. Boil the wheat-flour noodles for 5 mins or if using spaghetti boil it for 15–18 mins and then drain. You will need to make more sauce by adding 450 ml (¾ pint) of stock. To make vegetarian stock, add 100 g (¼ lb) shredded carrots, 100 g (¼ lb) mushroom stalks, and a medium-sized chopped up onion to 900 ml (1½ pints) of water to which a vegetarian stock cube has been added. Boil until the liquid has been reduced by half. Follow the previous recipe, adding an additional 1½ tbs of light soya sauce. Add the extra stock 10 mins before the end of the cooking time and the wheat-flour noodles, 5 mins before the end.

Serving
Divide the cooked noodles between 4 serving bowls or rice bowls, then add the soup. Eat the noodles in the Chinese style with chop-sticks. (You may need to lift the bowl to your mouth!)

Peking Boiled Noodles in Minced Meat Sauce *(for 3–4 people)*

- 450 g (1 lb) Chinese noodles or spaghetti
- 5–6 medium Chinese dried mushrooms
- 1 medium-sized onion
- 2–3 stalks spring onion
- 20 cm (8 in) piece of cucumber
- 3 tbs vegetable oil
- 350–450 g (¾ –1 lb) minced pork or beef
- 1 tsp salt
- pepper (to taste)
- 2 tbs soya sauce paste
- 1½ tbs dark soya sauce
- 2 tbs dry sherry
- 1½ tbs cornflour (blended in 4 tbs cold water)

Preparation
Boil the noodles for 5 mins or the spaghetti for 15–18 mins. Drain and rinse under running water to separate them. Soak the mushrooms in 8 tbs of boiling water for 20

mins. Drain, reserving the mushroom water. Coarsely chop the caps of the mushrooms, discarding the stalks. Chop the onion into similar sized pieces and cut the spring onions into 5 cm (2 in) lengths and the cucumber into double matchstick-sized strips.

Cooking
Heat the oil in a wok. When hot stir-fry the onions and mushrooms together for 1½ mins. Add minced meat, salt and pepper and continue to stir-fry over a medium heat for 4–5 mins. Add soya sauce paste, soya sauce, mushroom water and sherry. Continue to cook together for 5 mins. Add the blended cornflour and stir and turn until the sauce thickens. Cook for 1½ mins.

Serving
Reheat the pasta by placing it on a colander and pouring a kettleful of boiling water through it. Let it drain well. Transfer to a large deep-sided serving dish. Pour the meat sauce from the wok over the centre of the noodles. Surround with the freshly shredded cucumber and chopped spring onions. The diners should toss and mix the meat sauce with the noodles, cucumber and spring onions and then transfer a helping to their own bowls. You can eat this either in the Sino-Italian style of turning the noodles around your chopsticks or in the age-old Chinese style of lifting the bowl close to your mouth and simply shoving the noodles in with the help of chopsticks. Whichever method is used, this is very satisfying food to tuck into.

Quick-fried Noodles (or Chow Mien) with Shredded Meat and Vegetables *(for 3–4 people)*

This is a versatile dish which can be cooked with any meat (pork, beef, lamb or chicken) cooked or fresh or with seafoods (shrimps, prawns or crab meat) or both. You will need two woks for it.

  4 rashers bacon
  1 tbs dried shrimps
  4 large Chinese mushrooms
  150–175 g (5–6 oz) broccoli
  1 medium-sized onion
  2 stalks spring onion
  2 slices root-ginger
  450 g (1 lb) Chinese noodles or spaghetti
  5 tbs vegetable oil
  ½ tsp salt
  2 cloves garlic
  4–5 fresh or frozen shrimps
  1½ tbs soya sauce
  1 tbs oyster sauce
  4 tbs good stock
  1½ tbs dry sherry

Preparation
Derind the bacon and cut it into matchstick-sized shreds. Soak the shrimps and mushrooms together in boiling water for 20 mins. Drain and reserve the liquid. Cut the mushroom caps and shrimps into matchstick-sized shreds. Discard the stalks. Cut broccoli into a dozen pieces. Slice the onion thinly and cut the spring onions into 2.5 cm (1 in) sections. Crush and chop the ginger coarsely. Parboil the broccoli with the noodles for 5 mins or the spaghetti for 16 mins and drain. Place them in a wok with 1 tbs oil.

Cooking
Heat 3½ tbs oil in another wok. When hot add the bacon, ginger, dried shrimps, mushrooms and sliced onions. Stir-fry over a medium heat for 3 mins. Add the mushroom and shrimp water and salt. Bring to the boil

and simmer gently for 3 mins. Pour two-thirds of this mixture over the noodles and broccoli in the first wok and turn them over a gentle heat. Meanwhile, add the remaining oil to the second wok together with the garlic, spring onion and shrimps. Bring to a rapid boil. Add soya sauce, oyster sauce, stock and sherry. Stir-fry them over high heat for 1½ mins. Spoon half the contents of this wok into the wok with the noodles and broccoli, stir and turn vigorously over high heat for 1 min. Place in a large deep-sided serving dish. Pour the contents of the second wok over the noodles in the dish as a garnish.

Serving
Bring the serving dish to the table for the diners to help themselves. This dish will be eaten in the same way as the previous recipe.

East China

INTRODUCTION

East China and the Lower Yangtze are a well-watered region, so there is an abundance of vegetables and fresh-water produce. In the traditional division of Chinese culinary regions, the area is usually further divided into two parts: the North Yangtze regions, which are designated the Huai-Yang region (Huai for the Huai River and Yang for the city of Yangchow), and the Chang Nan Region, or the South of the River region, where you find the cities of Nanking, Soochow, Hangchow and Shanghai. All these towns and cities are on the tourist maps of China these days, ever since the country was opened up to foreign tourists a few years ago. When we winged our way down from the North during our gastronomic tours of China, we managed to stay a few days each in every one of these cities and we ate in as many places as time would allow.

The Lower Yangtze is distinctly different from the North in that this is not cattle-raising country and therefore there is far less beef and lamb on the table; nor are meats so often roasted or barbecued. Vegetables there are in plenty: lotus leaves are used frequently (almost like tin foil in the West) to wrap foods before steaming, baking or simmering them. Lotus roots are often served as a feature of vegetable dishes. The salted green mustard pickles, called 'Snow Pickles', are used more widely than elsewhere in providing flavouring for both fish and meat dishes. Bean curd also is more widely used here than anywhere else, whether in the form of pressed bean curd, bean curd skin or fresh bean curd, lightly poached. This unique Chinese food material is often cooked with vegetables, meat or fish. It is an important addition to the diet of anyone inclined towards vegetarianism. When salted and fermented it becomes a kind of 'cheese' which is used extensively for the flavouring of both meats and vegetables.

Like lotus roots, bamboo shoots are used more extensively than in the North. There are always bamboo groves and mulberry trees (the leaves feed silkworms) around farm houses. The shoots are often cooked with dried mushrooms so that the intensified flavour of the mushrooms will mingle with the much more subtle and less pronounced flavour of the bamboo shoots. All along the railway track from Nanking to Shanghai, a distance of over 150 miles, the landscape is dotted with well-built houses with high chimneys. On enquiring what these latter were, I was told that mushrooms are force-grown and later dried in these houses. There seems to be a great shortage of Chinese mushrooms throughout the world; anyone who has purchased them will have noticed that they are a prohibitive price. Yet they are essential in creating that typical Chinese flavour (especially when used in conjunction with dried shrimps) which the Chinese expect.

As we travelled around the region I found Yangchow on the northern bank of the Yangtze to be a very peaceful city, although it is the site of the infamous nineteenth-century massacre when Manchu Government troops re-occupied it from the Taiping rebels. There is a long, lazy, tranquil lake right in the middle of the city which can be viewed from the Yangchow Hotel through a moon-shaped window. It was here that we had one of the best meals of our whole tour. This was the menu:

Appetizers
Dried Velveteen of 'Meat Wool'
Cold Sliced Roast Duck
Pickled Ginger
Hot Rice-Cake Diamonds
Sliced Pickled Cucumber
Green Beans in Savoury Sauce and Sesame Oil
Braised Eel in Soya Sauce
Steamed Shrimps
Quick-fried Shredded Pressed Bean Curd
Soya-Braised Bamboo Shoots

Main Dishes
Quick-fried Prawns on Sizzling Rice

A Trio of Stuffed Pastries
   Stuffed Marrow with Meat and Radish
   Sesame Baked Buns with Black Bean Fillings
   Rice with Yellow Beans

Crispy Miniature Spring Rolls with Fish and Spring Onion
Hairy Rivercrabs Baked in Shells (with roe and ginger)
Paper-wrapped Deep-fried Chicken
Fish Fu-Yung with Carrots
Crispy Mandarin 'Squirrel Fish'
Stir-fried Green Beans with Mushrooms
Stuffed Lotus Roots with Plum Sauce
Turtle and Bamboo Shoot Soup (served in individual stoneware pots)

This menu immediately confirms that the food in this region is not heavy with meat, but that there is a profusion of fish, vegetables and freshwater crustaceans. Two fish which are frequently seen on the table are eels and turtles, and while in the North there are large prawns, here on the Yangtze there are small freshwater shrimps in abundance, which are particularly suitable for frying in a wok. Freshwater shrimps and crabs are often eaten cooked on their own or in conjunction with vegetables and meats. (For instance, there is a well-known Yangtze riverside dish called Chingkiang 'Crab meat Lion's Head Meatball'.)

Having given you a small sample of the flavour of East China, I shall now proceed to lead you into cooking some of the dishes of the region in a wok.

SOUPS

Three Chopped and Three Shredded Ingredients Soup *(for 4–6 people)*

50–75 g (2–3 oz) ham
50–75 g (2–3 oz) cooked chicken
2 stalks spring onion
3 slices root-ginger
40 g (1½ oz) Ja Tsai Pickles
40 g (1½ oz) Chinese dried shrimps
1.1 litres (2 pints) good stock
1 chicken stock cube
salt and pepper (to taste)
1 tsp sesame oil

Preparation
Cut the ham and chicken into double-sized matchsticks and the spring onions into 5 cm (2 in) pieces. Coarsely chop the ginger and pickle. Soak the dried shrimps in 6 tbs of boiling water for 15 mins. Drain and reserve the shrimp water. Chop the shrimps up coarsely.

Cooking
Heat the stock in a wok. Add the ginger, pickle and shrimps. Bring to the boil and simmer gently for 5–6 mins.

Stir and add the stock cube, chicken, ham and the shrimp water. Continue to simmer for 3–4 mins. Season to taste with salt and pepper. Finally, sprinkle the soup with spring onions and sesame oil. Serve.

Serving
Serve in a large soup bowl and drink throughout the meal.

Yangchow Main Course Chicken Soup *(for 4–8 people)*

1.6 kg (3½ lb) chicken
1 pair pig's trotters
3 slices root-ginger
150–175 g (5–6 oz) bamboo shoots
2 stalks spring onion
salt and pepper (to taste)
225 g (½ lb) ham
900 ml (1½ pints) good stock
2 chicken stock cubes
900 ml (1½ pints) water

Preparation
Parboil the chicken and trotters for 10 mins and drain. Cut the ginger into thin slices and the bamboo shoots into 5 cm (2 in) thick triangular-shaped pieces and the spring onions into 5 cm (2 in) pieces.

Cooking
Heat water in a wok. When it boils add the chicken, trotters, ginger and salt. Bring to the boil and simmer gently for 45 mins (keep adding water to the wok so as to keep the volume constant). Add the ham, bamboo shoots, stock and stock cubes. Continue simmering for ½ hour. Adjust the seasoning with salt and pepper.

Serving

Pour into a large soup bowl or tureen, sprinkle with spring onions and bring to the table. This soup should be drunk and eaten throughout the meal. This is one of those Chinese 'semi-soup' dishes, which serves the purpose of being both a soup as well as a main course dish. When serving such a dish you can reduce the main course dishes by one. The chicken and trotters in the soup should be tender enough to be dismembered easily or taken to pieces with a pair of chop-sticks. Pieces of them should be dipped in a dipping sauce before being eaten. Use the same dipping sauce as for Pork Spare-rib and Cucumber Soup but add 1 tbs of chilli sauce.

Four-Colour Soup *(for 4–5 people)*

   100 g (¼ lb) dried lotus seeds
   100 g (¼ lb) cooked chicken meat
   100 g (¼ lb) ham
   75 g (3 oz) pressed bean curd (optional)
   2 slices root-ginger
   2 tbs lard
   900 ml (1½ pints) good stock
   1 chicken stock cube
   100 g (¼ lb) peas (fresh or frozen)
   salt and pepper (to taste)
   1½ tbs cornflour (blended in 4 tbs water)
   1 tsp sesame oil

Preparation
Soak the lotus seeds overnight. Drain and blanch in plenty of water for 10 mins. Finely dice the chicken meat, ham and pressed bean curd. Coarsely chop the ginger.

Cooking
Heat the lard in a wok. When it is hot add the ginger, lotus

seeds and stir-fry for 3 mins. Add the ham, chicken and bean curd and continue stir-frying for another 2 mins. Pour in the stock, crumble in the stock cube and add the peas. Season with salt and pepper. Stir in the blended cornflour. Cook for 1 min. Sprinkle with sesame oil and serve.

Serving
Pour into a large soup bowl. Like the previous dish, this is a useful dish to lend weight to a meal as it can be ladled into individual rice bowls and be eaten with rice. It is also a colourful dish which will add colour to the spread on the table.

Fish Head and Bean Curd Main Course Soup *(for 4–6 people)*

1 large freshwater fish head
100 g (¼ lb) ham or gammon
4 stalks spring onion
4 slices root-ginger
1–1½ bean curd cakes
1½ chicken stock cubes
300 ml (½ pint) milk
salt and pepper (to taste)
2 tbs white wine

Preparation
Clean and chop the fish head vertically in half. Parboil in boiling water for 5 mins and drain. Cut the gammon or ham into a dozen pieces, the spring onion into 5 cm (2 in) lengths (keep the white and the green parts separate) and the ginger into thin slices. Cut the bean curd into sugar lump-sized pieces.

Cooking

Place the pieces of fish head and the ginger in the bottom of a wok. Pour in 900 ml (1½ pints) water, bring to the boil and simmer gently for 15 mins. Add the ham, stock cube and the whites of the spring onions. Continue simmering for 15 mins. Add the milk, bean curd and adjust the seasoning with salt and pepper. Two mins after it has reboiled, sprinkle with the green parts of the spring onion and white wine and serve.

Serving

This is another substantial soup which can act as a main course dish as well as a soup.

You can make it stretch even further, if an unexpected guest arrives, by adding an extra ½ cake of bean curd.

Spinach and Bean Curd Soup with Shredded Ham *(for 4–6 people)*

225 g (½ lb) spinach
2 bean curd cakes
100 g (¼ lb) smoked ham
900 ml (1½ pints) good stock
1 chicken stock cube
salt and pepper (to taste)
1 tsp sesame oil

Preparation

Clean the spinach thoroughly. Blanch in boiling water for ¼ min and drain. Cut the bean curd into sugar lump-sized cubes. Cut the ham into fine matchsticks.

Cooking

Bring the stock to boil in a wok. Add crumbled stock cube. When it dissolves, add the spinach, bean curd and ham. When it comes to the boil again reduce the heat and leave to simmer gently for 5 mins. Season to taste with salt and pepper. Sprinkle with sesame oil and serve.

Serving
Serve in a large soup bowl and eat throughout the meal. Although light and simple, this soup is very nourishing.

Whole Fish Soup *(for 4–8 people)*

- 2 lb whole fish (carp, trout, bass, perch etc.)
- salt and pepper (to taste)
- 2 tbs cornflour
- 3 stalks spring onion
- 2 tbs parsley or coriander leaves
- 4 tbs vegetable oil
- 3 slices root-ginger
- 900 ml (1½ pints) good stock
- 1 chicken stock cube
- 2 tbs dry sherry
- 2 tbs vinegar
- 1½ tbs light soya sauce
- 1 tsp sesame oil

Preparation
Clean the fish thoroughly and score deeply 3–4 times on either side. Rub evenly with salt, pepper and cornflour. Cut the spring onions into 2.5 cm (1 in) pieces, separating the white and green parts. Chop the parsley or fresh coriander.

Cooking
Heat oil in a wok. When it is very hot add the ginger and the whites of the spring onion. Turn and stir them around a few times to flavour the oil. Add the fish and fry it for 1½ mins on both sides. Pour in the stock and add the crumbled stock cube. Simmer gently for 10 mins. Add the

sherry, vinegar and soya sauce. Turn the fish over a couple of times. Garnish with the green parts of the spring onions, chopped parsley or coriander leaves and sprinkle on the sesame oil.

Serving
Serve in an oval tureen or oval deep-sided dish. A refreshing semi-soup with a distinctive flavour, very reminiscent of the South Yangtze.

Crab Meat, Bean Curd and Lotus Seed Soup *(for 4 people)*

  350 g (¾ lb) dried lotus seeds
  225 g (½ lb) crab meat (cooked or canned)
  2 slices root-ginger
  2 cloves garlic
  2 stalks spring onion
  1 bean curd cake
  2 tbs vegetable oil
  salt and pepper (to taste)
  900 ml (1½ pints) good stock
  1 chicken stock cube
  2 tbs cornflour (blended in 6 tbs cold water)
  1 tbs white wine

Preparation
Soak the lotus seeds overnight. Drain. Cover with water and boil for 15 mins. Drain. Flake the crab meat. Coarsely chop the ginger and garlic. Thinly slice the spring onions, separating the green and white parts. Cut the bean curd cake into small sugar lump-sized pieces.

Cooking
Heat the oil in a wok. When it is hot add the garlic, ginger, the white of the spring onions, the crab meat and salt. Stir-fry for ½ min over a medium heat. Add the stock,

lotus seeds and stock cube. Bring to the boil and simmer gently for 10 mins. Add the bean curd pieces. Season to taste with salt and pepper. When it has boiled again for 2 mins, stir in the blended cornflour to thicken. Finally sprinkle with white wine and the green parts of the spring onion.

Serving
This is a very flavoursome soup, which can be served to counterbalance any heavy meat dish.

'Proletarian' Yellow Bean and Shredded Pork Soup (for 4–5 people)

225 g (½ lb) yellow beans (soya beans)
2 medium-sized onions
225 g (½ lb) pork (lean and fat)
2–3 tbs chopped parsley or spring onion (or both)
2 tbs vegetable oil
2 tbs light soya sauce
900 ml (1½ pints) stock
salt and pepper (to taste)
1½ tbs lard

Preparation
Soak the yellow beans for 24 hours. Chop the onions and put them in a blender with the beans. Blend for 1 min. Chop the pork into coarse mince-like pieces. Finely chop the parsley and/or spring onions.

Cooking
Heat the oil in a wok. When it is hot add the pork and stir-fry over a medium heat for 3 mins. Add the blended beans and onions. Continue stir-frying for another 2 mins. Pour in 150 ml (¼ pint) of water and the soya sauce and bring to the boil. Simmer and stir gently for 15 mins. Add

the stock and adjust the seasoning with salt and pepper. Bring to the boil and keep boiling for 5 mins. Add the lard and sprinkle with parsley and/or spring onions.

Serving
Serve in a large soup bowl. This is a useful dish to serve to lend weight to a meal as it can be ladled into individual rice bowls and eaten with rice.

Pork, Mushroom, Marrow and Asparagus Soup *(for 4 to 5 people)*

100 g (¼ lb) lean pork
salt and pepper (to taste)
1½ tbs cornflour
½ egg white
6 medium Chinese dried mushrooms
225 g (½ lb) marrow
2–3 sticks asparagus
2 tbs vegetable oil
1.1 litres (2 pints) good stock
1 chicken stock cube
150 g (5 oz) button mushrooms

Preparation
Cut the pork into very thin slices about 2.5 × 3.5 cm (1 × 1½ in). Rub with salt, cornflour and wet with egg white. Soak the dried mushrooms in 8 tbs of hot water for 20 mins. Drain and reserve the mushroom water. Discard the stems and cut the caps into quarters. Peel away the marrow skin and cut the marrow into 12 equal-sized pieces. Remove the tough root ends of the asparagus and cut each stick slantwise into 6 pieces. Boil for 5 mins and drain.

Cooking

Heat the oil in a wok. When hot stir-fry the pork slices in it for 1 min. Set to one side. Add the stock and bring to the boil. Add the stock cube and all the other ingredients except the pork. When it boils again reduce the heat and leave to simmer gently for 15 mins. Return the pork to the wok and season to taste with salt and pepper. Simmer for another 2 mins and serve.

Serving

Although this soup is full of vegetables it is a light, clear soup and should be eaten partly as a vegetable dish and partly as a soup throughout the meal.

Pork Spare-rib and Cucumber Soup *(for 4–6 people)*

700 g (1½ lb) pork spare-ribs
15 cm (6 in) piece cucumber
2 stalks spring onion
3 slices root-ginger
1.1 litres (2 pints) good stock
1 chicken stock cube
salt and pepper (to taste)

Preparation

Cut spare-ribs into individual ribs and then in half. Boil vigorously for 5–6 mins and drain. Cut the cucumber into double-sized matchsticks and the spring onions into 5 cm (2 in) pieces.

Cooking

Heat the stock in a wok. Add the ribs and ginger and bring to the boil. Reduce heat to very low and simmer gently for ½ hour. Add the stock cube, cucumber and finally the spring onion and season to taste with salt and pepper.

Serving

Serve in a large bowl and eat or drink it throughout the meal. Diners can extract the ribs from the soup and dip them individually into dipping sauces before eating. The meat on the ribs should be tender enough to tear off easily from the bone. You can make a good dipping sauce by mixing together 4 tbs soya sauce with 2 tbs vinegar, 1 tbs chopped garlic and 1 tbs chopped root-ginger.

RICE

Yangchow Fried Rice *(for 4–6 people)*

Yangchow Fried Rice is probably the best known fried rice dish in China. Fried rice is a dish which can be made by stir-frying together leftover rice with any leftover savoury bits and pieces. In China, 'fried rice' is seldom prepared from freshly cooked rice, but there is nothing to stop you from doing this. I think that the reason why this Yangchow version is so famous is that the shrimps in it give it a special appeal. Small shrimps are readily available in the Yangchow region. However, the real success of fried rice depends on it having a salty ingredient (such as bacon, ham or salted fish) as well as a quantity of diced vegetables which counterbalance the blandness of the rice.

- 450 g (1 lb) cooked rice
- 4 tbs vegetable oil
- 3 rashers bacon
- 4 stalks spring onion
- 2 medium-sized tomatoes
- 5 tbs peas (fresh or frozen)
- ½ tsp salt
- 2 tbs butter or lard
- 225 g (½ lb) peeled shrimps (fresh or frozen)

East China

400 g (14 oz) can of champignon or fresh button mushrooms
2 tbs light soya sauce

Preparation
Warm the rice in 1 tbs of the oil over a low heat in a wok. Derind the bacon and cut across the lean and fat parts, making thin shreds. Cut each spring onion down the middle and separate the green and white parts. Finely chop each part. Cut each tomato into 8–10 pieces.

Cooking
Heat 3 tbs of oil in a wok. When it is hot add the whites of the spring onions and the bacon. Stir them together over high heat for 1 min. Add the peas, sprinkle them with salt and continue stir-frying for another min. Turn the heat to very low. Mix the rice into the wok and stir everything together, turning the mixture a couple of times so it is evenly mixed.

Melt the butter (or lard) in the empty wok and add the shrimps, mushrooms and tomatoes. Increase the heat to high. Stir-fry gently for 1½ mins and add to the rice mixture in the other wok. Mix the ingredients well.

Serving
Sprinkle the fried rice with soya sauce and the green parts of the spring onions. Serve. This is a delectable dish which can either be eaten on its own or with other dishes.

Ham and Egg Fried Rice *(for 4–6 people)*

The region is well known for its famous Ching-hua ham, which is often used to enhance the flavour of Fried Rice. Eggs can also be added to enrich Fried Rice. The richness of these ingredients is counterbalanced by the other vegetable ingredients which are also used.

450 g (1 lb) cooked rice
5 tbs vegetable oil
4 stalks spring onion
4 eggs
1 tsp salt
2 sticks celery
15 cm (6 in) piece of cucumber
1 red pepper
100 g (¼ lb) ham
2 tbs butter (or lard)
2 tbs light soya sauce

Preparation
Warm the rice in 1 tbs of oil over a low heat in a large wok. Separate the white and green parts of the spring onions. Cut each section coarsely. Beat the eggs lightly with salt. Cut the celery into 6 mm (¼ in) lengths and the cucumber and pepper into 6 mm (¼ in) slices. Cut the ham into similar-sized pieces.

Cooking
Heat the remaining oil in a smaller wok. Add the whites of the spring onions and the ham. Stir and turn them around for ½ min and push them to one side of the wok. Pour the beaten eggs into the centre and allow them to fry steadily for a quarter of a min. Push them around so as to allow the liquid parts of the egg to flow to the bottom and cook more evenly. After ½ min bring the ham and spring onion into the centre of the wok and mix and scramble them with the egg. When nearly all the egg has set, empty it into the wok containing the rice.

Put the heat on low while you stir and turn the rice and egg mixture.

Melt the butter in the smaller wok. Add the celery, pepper and cucumber. Turn the heat to high and stir-fry for ½ min. Empty into the rice mixture and amalgamate all the ingredients well.

Serving
Sprinkle the top of the rice with soya sauce and the chopped green parts of the spring onion. Serve. This is another delectable dish which can be eaten on its own or with other dishes.

Fried Rice with Fresh Fish and Salt Fish *(for 6 people)*

You will need two woks for this dish.

2 stalks spring onion
40 g (1½ oz) Chinese green mustard pickle, 'Snow Pickles' or gherkins
2 medium-sized carrots
3 eggs (hard-boiled)
1 medium-sized onion
175 g (6 oz) fresh fillet of fish
4 tbs vegetable oil
75 g (3 oz) dried salted fish
450 g (1 lb) cooked rice
2 tbs lard (or butter)
2 tbs soya sauce
1½ tbs dry sherry

Preparation
Chop the spring onion coarsely and the pickle finely. Cut the carrots and hard-boiled eggs into 1 cm (½ in) cubes. Slice the onions. Parboil and flake the fresh fish. Heat 3 tbs oil over a medium heat and cook the salted fish for 2–3 mins on either side until almost crisp. Chop coarsely.

Put the cooked rice into a wok. Turn the fish in it and mix well.

Cooking

Heat the remaining oil together with the lard (or butter) in a wok. When hot add onions and carrots. Stir-fry them for 1½ mins. Add flaked fish, pickle and peas. Stir-fry them with the other ingredients for 1½ mins. Turn them all into the wok containing the rice and salt fish mixture. Add the chopped eggs. Turn and toss them all together until well mixed.

Serving

Sprinkle the contents of the wok with soya sauce, sherry and chopped spring onion. Serve. This is an extremely satisfying dish which can be eaten on its own (not unlike kedgeree) or with just one or two supplementary dishes (e.g. a vegetable dish and/or a bean curd dish).

Fish and Dried Shrimp Soft Rice (Congee) *(for 4–5 people)*

This dish is often served in the Eastern region for breakfast or as a late-night supper.

3 rashers bacon
3 slices root-ginger
1½ tbs dried shrimps
450 g (1 lb) cooked rice
2 chicken stock cubes
1 tsp salt
225 g (½ lb) filleted white fish (cod, plaice, sole, halibut, etc.)
4 tbs peas
100 g (¼ lb) bean sprouts
4 tbs roasted peanuts
2 tbs soya sauce
1 tsp sesame oil

Preparation

Cut bacon across lean and fat. Finely chop the ginger into shreds. Soak the dried shrimps in hot water for 15 mins.

Cooking

Place the cooked rice in a wok, pour in 1.7 litres (3 pints) water and bring to the boil. Add the dried shrimps and bacon, reduce the heat and leave to simmer gently, uncovered, for 45 mins. Stir now and again. Add the stock cubes, salt, fish and peas into the rice and continue to simmer gently for another 10 mins. Add bean sprouts and peanuts and cook gently for another 5 mins.

Serving

Transfer the contents of the wok into a large bowl or tureen. Sprinkle with soya sauce and sesame oil and let the diners help themselves.

Vegetarian Fried Rice *(for 4–5 people)*

- 1 cake bean curd
- vegetable oil for deep frying
- 40 g (1½ oz) Chinese green mustard pickle, 'Snow Pickles'
- 40 g (1½ oz) Chinese 'Winter Pickle' (optional)
- 25 g (1 oz) Ja Tsai Pickles
- 1 medium-sized onion
- 75 g (3 oz) lotus nuts
- 2 medium-sized new carrots
- 75 g (3 oz) bamboo shoots
- 100 g (¼ lb) small button mushrooms
- 125–150 g (4–5 oz) courgettes
- 1 medium-sized green pepper
- 1 medium-sized red pepper
- 450 g (1 lb) cooked rice
- 3 tbs lard (or butter)

1 tbs bean curd 'cheese' (optional)
1½ tbs sherry
2 medium-sized tomatoes
50 g (2 oz) fresh or frozen peas
2½ tbs soya sauce
1½ tsp sesame oil

Preparation
Cut the bean curd cake into 20 pieces. Heat the vegetable oil and deep-fry the bean curd cake pieces in it for 1½ mins. Drain. Chop the three types of pickles and onion coarsely. Boil the lotus nuts for 20 mins. Drain. Cut the carrots and bamboo shoots into 6 mm (¼ in) cubes. Cut each mushroom through the stem into quarters, the courgettes into 6 mm (¼ in) lengths and the peppers into 12 mm (½ in) pieces.

Cooking
Heat 4–5 tbs of oil in a wok. When hot add the carrots, nuts and onion. Stir-fry over medium heat for 2 mins. Add the pickles and continue to stir and turn them together for 1 min. Add the bean curd cubes and stir-fry for ½ min. Put the cooked rice into a wok, add all the stir-fried vegetables to it and mix together. Keep hot over a low heat. Heat the lard (or butter) in another wok over medium heat. When it has melted add the bean curd 'cheese', sherry and 4 tbs of water. Mash them together for a ¼ min as they boil. Now add the remaining vegetables: courgettes, peppers, mushrooms, bamboo shoots and tomatoes. Turn them over a high heat for 1½ mins. Reduce the heat to low and allow the vegetables to simmer together for 2 mins. Turn the contents of this wok into the other wok. Stir, turn and toss together until they are all well mixed.

Serving

Turn the contents out onto a very large and well-heated dish or bowl. Sprinkle with soya sauce and sesame oil and serve. This is a large and satisfying dish, enough for at least 4–6 hungry mouths. It will appeal to vegetarians and non-vegetarians alike.

NOODLES

Shanghai Cold-tossed Noodles *(for 4 people)*

The ingredients for this dish are inexpensive. It is a favourite lunch dish for the average housewife on the Lower Yangtze. Although a simple dish it is one that often appeals to the connoisseur. There is no 'loss of face' even if it is served as a starter at a good class dinner party.

450 (1 lb) Chinese noodles (large size) or spaghetti
¼ chicken stock cube
3 tbs stock
2 tbs light soya sauce
1½ tbs vegetable oil
3 stalks spring onion
1½ tbs dried shrimps
40 g (1½ oz) green mustard pickle, 'Snow Pickles' or substitute 50 g (2 oz) gherkins
1½ tbs sesame oil
1½ tbs peanut butter
100 g (¼ lb) bean sprouts
1 tbs dark soya sauce
1 tbs wine vinegar
1 tbs dry sherry

Preparation
Boil the Chinese noodles for 8 mins or spaghetti for 15–18 mins. Drain thoroughly and place in a wok. Dissolve the stock cube thoroughly in the stock. Sprinkle it together with the light soya sauce and vegetable oil evenly over the noodles. Turn and toss the noodles so that the ingredients are evenly mixed. Coarsely chop the spring onions. Meanwhile, soak the dried shrimps for 20 mins. Drain and chop up finely. Finely chop the pickles. Stir the sesame oil into the peanut butter and dot the top of the noodles with it. Sprinkle evenly with the pickles and dried shrimps. Boil the bean sprouts for 10 seconds and pile in a mound at the centre of the noodles. Sprinkle the bean sprouts with dark soya sauce, vinegar and sherry and the surrounding noodles with the chopped spring onions.

Serving
Serve by bringing the wok to the table (it is best to use a two-handled wok and let the diners toss and mix the noodles and other ingredients together).

Chingkiang Riverside Noodles *(for 4 people)*

The riverside is cold on the Lower Yangtze in the winter and there is little domestic heat anywhere, certainly no central heating. People wear thick padded gowns and jackets. Substantial noodle-soup dishes, such as this, give great comfort and 'stoke up the heat' which will last for some hours inside the heavy clothing. It could do the same for the residents of Northern Europe and America. It is, in fact, a very tasty and satisfying dish to have anywhere at any time of the year.

For Stock
1 fish head (about 600–700 g/1¼–1½ lb)
1 fish tail (about 225 g/½ lb)

1 medium-sized onion
3 slices root-ginger
2 tbs dried shrimps
1 chicken stock cube
1 tsp salt
pepper (to taste)

For Noodles
450 g (1 lb) large Chinese noodles or spaghetti
225–350 g (½–¾ lb) filleted fish (bass, trout, cod, halibut etc.)
8 medium-sized Chinese dried mushrooms
100–150 g (4–5 oz) firm button mushrooms
2 rashers bacon
75 g (3 oz) bamboo shoots (optional)
2 stalks spring onion
15 g (½ oz) Ja Tsai Pickles
3 tbs vegetable oil
1 tbs lard
2 tbs soya sauce
1½ tsp sugar
1½ tsp dry sherry

Preparation
Clean the fish head and tail and place them at the bottom of a wok. Pour in 1.4 litres (2½ pints) of cold water. Slice the onion and add it with the ginger and dried shrimps to the wok. Bring to the boil and simmer gently for 30 mins. Add the stock cube, salt and pepper. Stir and continue simmering for 5–6 mins. Strain the stock into a large bowl. Prepare the noodles by boiling them for 8 mins, if you are using spaghetti it will take 16 mins; drain thoroughly. Cut the filleted fish into 2.5 × 1 cm (1 × ½ in) pieces. Soak the dried mushrooms in hot water for 20 mins. Drain. Discard the mushroom stems and cut caps into quarters. Clean and cut the button mushrooms through the stems into quar-

ters; cut the bacon across the lean and fat into shreds; cut the bamboo shoots into double-sized matchstick shreds and the spring onion into 5 cm (2 in) lengths. Finely chop the pickles.

Cooking

Heat the oil in a wok. When hot add the pieces of fish and turn them over a few times. Fry them for about 20 secs. Remove with a slotted spoon and put aside. Add the lard. When it has melted add the dried mushrooms, pickle, bamboo shoots and bacon. Stir-fry them over a high heat for 1 min. Add the fresh mushrooms and continue stir-frying for another min. Return the fried fish to the wok and sprinkle it with soya sauce, sugar and sherry. Cook, stirring for ½ min.

Serving

Divide the noodles between 4 large rice bowls. Reboil the stock and adjust the seasoning. Pour it over the noodles in the bowls. Heat the wok ingredients and divide them between the bowls.

Three Shrimp Cooked Noodles *(for 4 people)*

225 g (½ lb) fresh or frozen unshelled shrimps
2 tbs vegetable oil
8 large prawns
3 slices root-ginger
salt and pepper
1½ tbs dried shrimps
4 stalks spring onion
450 g (1 lb) noodles (or spaghetti)
900 ml (1½ pints) good stock
1½ chicken stock cubes
1½ tbs Chinese shrimp sauce
1½ tbs vinegar

½ tbs lard
3 cloves garlic
2 tbs soya sauce
1 tbs hoisin sauce
½ tsp sugar
1½ tbs dry sherry

Preparation
Clean the fresh or frozen shrimps thoroughly. Remove their heads, tails and shells. Heat the oil in a wok and place the heads, tail and shells in it and heat for ¼ min. Do the same with the heads and tails of the prawns. Add the ginger, salt and pepper and stir-fry over a medium heat for 1 min. Pour in 900 ml (1½ pints) of water and bring to the boil. Soak the dried shrimps in hot water for 20 mins. Drain them and add to the wok. Cut the spring onion into 2.5 cm (1 in) lengths. Separate the white and green parts. Add half the white parts to the stock liquid and leave to simmer for 20 mins. Strain the stock and discard all the strained ingredients.

Meanwhile, boil the noodles for 5 mins or if using spaghetti boil it for 10 mins. Drain and place at the bottom of a wok. Pour in all except for 3–4 tbs of the freshly prepared stock. Bring to the boil. Add the stock cube, season to taste with salt and pepper, add the shrimp sauce, and vinegar. Leave to simmer gently for 5 mins.

Cooking
Heat the lard in a separate wok. When hot add the garlic, the rest of the whites of the spring onions and the prawns. Stir-fry over a medium heat for 1½ mins. Sprinkle with soya sauce, hoisin sauce, sugar and sherry. Stir-fry together for ½ min. Reduce the heat and turn the contents over gently until nearly all the sauce has evaporated.

Serving

Divide the noodles and soup between 4 large rice bowls. Place the large prawns and the green parts of the spring onions on top as a garnish. Add the remaining 3–4 tbs of stock to the wok in which the prawns had been cooking. Bring to the boil and pour the resultant sauce over the prawns and noodles in the bowls. The noodles and soup should be extremely savoury.

Three Shrimp Noodles or 'Shrimp Chow Mien' *(for 4 people)*

This is a very flavoursome dish to serve as a snack or to lend weight to a multi-course party meal.

450 g (1 lb) Chinese noodles or spaghetti
1½ tbs dried shrimps
6 medium dried Chinese mushrooms
1 medium-sized onion
2 rashers bacon
3 slices root-ginger
225 g (½ lb) fresh or frozen shrimps
4 tbs vegetable oil
salt and pepper (to taste)
1½ tbs light soya sauce
1½ tbs shrimp sauce

For Garnish
2 medium-sized courgettes
3 stalks spring onion
8 large prawns
3 cloves garlic
2 tbs lard (or butter)
1½ tbs soya sauce
2 tbs good stock
1 tbs dry sherry
1 tsp sesame oil

Preparation

Boil the noodles in the same way as in the 2 previous recipes and drain. Soak the dried shrimps and mushrooms in 7 tbs of boiling water for 20 mins. Strain the liquid and reserve. Chop the shrimps and mushrooms. Finely chop the onion, bacon and ginger. Shell the prawns and reserve the shells.

Cooking

Bring 5 tbs of the shrimp and mushroom water to the boil. 'Stir-fry' the prawn shells and heads in the liquid over a high heat for 1½-2 mins or until the liquid in the wok has been reduced to less than half. Remove the contents quickly with a slotted spoon. Add the mushrooms, soaked dried shrimps, onion, bacon, ginger and oil. Cook, stirring quickly over a high heat for 1 min. Add the fresh shrimps and cook, stirring for another min. Add the noodles or spaghetti. Turn them in the sauce over a medium heat. Season with salt, pepper, light soya sauce and shrimp sauce. Continue to turn and cook until the noodles are well heated through.

Meanwhile, prepare the 'garnish'. Cut the courgettes into 1 cm (½ in) lengths. Separate the white and green parts of the spring onions and finely chop each. Heat the lard (or butter) in a separate wok over a medium heat and add the courgettes. Stir them in the fat for 1 min over a high heat. Add the prawns, garlic and whites of the spring onions. Continue to stir-fry for another min. Pour in the soya sauce, stock and sherry. Turn the prawns and courgettes quickly in the sauce for a further ¾ min. Turn off the heat. Spoon half the contents into the wok containing the noodles and mix well.

Serving

Transfer the noodles etc. on to a well-heated deep-sided serving dish. Sprinkle with sesame oil and top them with the remainder of the prawn mixture from the second wok. Garnish with the green parts of the spring onions.

Pickle and Shredded Pork Noodles *(for 4 people)*

This is another simple but delicious noodle dish from the Lower Yangtze where pickles are widely used for heightening flavour.

    450 g (1 lb) noodles (or spaghetti)
    6 medium Chinese dried mushrooms
    50 g (2 oz) Chinese green mustard pickle ('Snow Pickles')
    2 stalks spring onions
    450 g (1 lb) pork (⅔ lean and ⅓ fat)
    2 medium-sized onions
    4 tbs vegetable oil
    2 tbs lard
    2 tbs light soya sauce
    2 tbs oyster sauce
    1 tbs dry sherry
    2 tbs good stock

Preparation
Boil the noodles or spaghetti as in the 3 previous recipes and drain. Soak the dried mushrooms in boiling water for 20 mins. Discard the stems and cut the caps into shreds. Coarsely chop the mustard pickle and cut the spring onions into 2.5 cm (1 in) lengths. Cut the pork across the lean and fat into double-sized matchstick pieces and the onion into thin slices.

Cooking
Heat the oil and lard in a wok. When it is hot add the onions, green mustard pickle, mushrooms and pork and stir-fry over a high heat for 3 mins. Add the soya sauce

and half the oyster sauce and continue to stir-fry over a high heat for a further min. Spoon half the contents, together with some of the flavoured oil, into another wok. Add the pasta and stir-fry over a medium heat for 1½ mins. Transfer into a large serving dish.

Serving
Add sherry, stock and spring onions into the first wok. Increase the heat to high and stir-fry for ½ min. Spoon, as a garnish, over the top of the noodle mixture in the serving dish. There is a savoury-sourness (due to the pickles) in this dish which gives it that very typical sharp taste of the region.

POULTRY

Shanghai Quick-braised Chicken on the bone *(for 6–8 people if served with rice and 1 or 2 other dishes)*

   1.5–1.6 kg (3–3½ lb) chicken
   2 stalks spring onion
   4 tbs vegetable oil
   3 slices root-ginger
   3 tbs soya sauce
   2 tbs yellow bean paste
   3 tsp sugar
   3 tbs dry sherry
   300 ml (½ pint) good stock
   1½ tbs cornflour (blended in 5 tbs cold water)
   1½ tbs lard

Preparation
Joint the chicken and chop through the bones into large bite-sized pieces. Blanch in boiling water for 3 mins and drain thoroughly. Cut the spring onion into 1 cm (½ in) thick slices.

Cooking

Heat the oil in a wok. When it is on the point of smoking, add the ginger and the chicken pieces. Turn them over and stir-fry for 4–5 mins. Add soya sauce, yellow bean paste, sugar and sherry. Stir to mix thoroughly. Pour in the stock and bring to a rapid boil over a high heat for about 15 mins. By this time the liquid in the wok should be reduced to less than a quarter of the original volume. Reduce the heat and carry on cooking the chicken gently in the sauce until the liquid has nearly dried out. Sprinkle evenly with the blended cornflour and add the lard. Turn the heat to high for a moment and stir, turning the mixture over rapidly. It is ready when the chicken pieces are coated by a rich shiny gloss of sauce. (It is the lard which helps give this sheen.)

Serving

Turn the chicken and sauce out on to a well-heated dish, sprinkle with the finely chopped spring onion and serve. Although comparatively simple this is a famous Shanghai dish which should take no more than 25 mins in all to cook. It is a highly appetizing dish which should appeal to all palates. This dish should be eaten with quantities of rice and vegetables. Wine can be served with it.

Drunken Chicken *(for 6–8 people, as a starter to a multi-course dinner party)*

- 1.6 kg (3½ lb) chicken
- 6 slices root-ginger
- 3 stalks spring onion
- ½ tsp five spice powder
- 4 tsp salt, pepper (to taste)
- 2 tbs brandy
- 150 ml (¼ pint) dry sherry

Preparation
Remove the legs and wings from the body of the chicken. Chop the body through the bones into 4 pieces. Put the chicken pieces into boiling water for 5 mins and drain. Cut up half the ginger finely and cut the spring onion into 2.5 cm (1 in) lengths, separating the white parts from the green parts.

Cooking
Heat 1.1 litres (2 pints) of water in a wok. Add half the salt, the uncut ginger, the white parts of the spring onion and the five spice powder. Put the chicken pieces in. Bring to the boil and leave to boil for 10 mins. Turn the heat off and allow the chicken pieces to cool in the water for 1 hour. Pour away the water and discard the used ginger and spring onion. Drain the chicken pieces and place them in a dish. Sprinkle them with the remaining chopped ginger, the green parts of the spring onions, the rest of the salt and some pepper. Turn the chicken pieces over a few times and leave to marinate in the basin for 3–4 hours. Now shake the chicken pieces free and discard the onion and ginger. Sprinkle the brandy over them and pour in the sherry. Turn the chicken over a few times and put in the refrigerator overnight to marinate in the winey mixture.

Serving
When you are about to serve, place the chicken pieces on a chopping board and chop through the bone into large bite-sized pieces. Arrange neatly on a plate and serve as an appetizer.

Quick-fried Chicken Slices with Bean Sprouts and Red Peppers *(for 4–6 people with 1 or 2 other dishes)*

    100 g (¼ lb) chicken breast meat
    ½ tsp salt

1½ tbs cornflour
½ egg white
2 stalks spring onion
1 medium-sized red pepper
225 g (½ lb) bean sprouts
5 tbs vegetable oil
2 tbs light soya sauce
2 tbs good stock
1½ tbs dry sherry
pepper (to taste)
1 tsp sesame oil

Preparation
Cut the chicken into 1 × 5 cm (½ × 2 in) thin slices. Sprinkle and rub with salt, cornflour and egg white. Cut the spring onion into 5 cm (2 in) pieces and the red pepper into the same sized strips as the chicken. Wash, drain and dry the bean sprouts.

Cooking
Heat 4 tbs of oil in a wok. When it is hot stir-fry the chicken pieces in it quickly over a high heat for 1 min. Remove with a slotted spoon and put aside. Add the remainder of the oil to the wok and stir-fry the spring onions, bean sprouts and peppers quickly over a high heat for 1 min. Add the soya sauce, stock and sherry and continue to stir-fry for another ½ min. Return the chicken pieces to the wok and stir-fry for another min. Season with pepper, sprinkle with sesame oil and serve.

Serving
Serve on a well-heated dish and eat hot from the wok. This is a good dish to serve with plain boiled rice. It is also good to nibble at while drinking wine.

Quick-fried Marinated Breast of Chicken (or duck) with Broccoli *(for 4–6 people with 1 or 2 dishes)*

225 g (½ lb) chicken (or duck) breast meat
½ tsp salt
pepper (to taste)
25 g (1 oz) white bean curd 'cheese'
4 tbs dry sherry
2 tbs cornflour
1 egg white
350 g (¾ lb) broccoli
4 tbs vegetable oil
3 tbs lard
2 cloves garlic
2 slices root-ginger
2 tbs soya sauce
4 tbs good stock

Preparation
Cut the chicken into 1 × 5 cm (½ × 2 in) thin slices. Rub the chicken slices evenly with salt and pepper, mash the bean curd 'cheese' with 2 tbs of the dry sherry and rub this into the chicken pieces too. Sprinkle with cornflour and wet with the egg white. Leave to marinate for 2–3 hours. Wash and cut the broccoli into pieces which are about 5 × 1.5 cm (2 × 1 in) long.

Cooking
Heat 1 tbs oil and 3 tbs of lard in a wok. When it is hot stir-fry the broccoli, garlic and ginger in it for 1½ mins. Add the soya sauce, good stock and the remaining sherry and continue to stir-fry for another 1½ mins. Reduce the heat to low, cover and allow the broccoli to steam for 3–4 mins. Remove the broccoli and arrange as a bed on a well-heated serving dish. Heat the remaining oil in another wok. Lift the handle so that the oil will grease the

surface of the wok evenly. Add the marinated chicken (or duck) pieces, laying them evenly in the wok. After 1½ mins turn them over and stir-fry them over a medium heat for another 1 min. Remove with slotted spoon and arrange them on top of the bed of broccoli and serve.

Serving
This is a dish of colourful white and green contrasts. It is good served with other brown coloured dishes which have a predominantly soya sauce flavour.

Quick-fried Chicken Cubes with Master Sauce, cooked Kidney and Liver on Crispy Noodles *(for 6–8 people with other dishes)*

   225 g (½ lb) breast of chicken
   225 g (½ lb) chicken liver
   225 g (½ lb) lamb's kidney
   15 cm (6 in) piece cucumber
   100 g (¼ lb) ham or gammon
   2–3 sprays fresh coriander
   100 g (¼ lb) rice flour vermicelli
   150 ml (¼ pint) vegetable oil
   300 ml (½ pint) Master Sauce (see page 154)
   1½ tbs soya sauce
   1½ tbs dry sherry
   4 tbs chicken stock
   ½ chicken stock cube
   1 tbs cornflour (blended in 4 tbs cold water)

Preparation
Cut the chicken breasts into small cubes. Remove the membranes and gristle from the liver and kidneys and cut them into similar-sized cubes. Heat 3 tbs of oil in a wok and stir-fry the liver and kidneys for 1 min. Remove and drain. Cut the cucumber and ham into the same sized

cubes. Chop the coriander. Boil the vermicelli for 2 mins. Drain. Heat the oil and plunge the noodles in it. They will crisp up almost immediately. When they do, remove with a slotted spoon and drain.

Cooking
Heat the Master Sauce in a wok. When it is hot add the chicken and ham or gammon cubes. Cook them together, stirring, for ½ min. Add soya sauce, dry sherry and chicken stock and crumbled stock cube, diced liver and kidneys and continue cooking and stirring the ingredients for another ½ min. Stir well and add the blended cornflour. Cook for a further min.

Serving
Put the crispy noodles on a dish and pour the chicken, gammon, liver and kidney sauce mixture over them. Garnish with chopped fresh coriander. This is a refined dish often served at parties. Its interest lies in the contrasting flavours and textures of the various ingredients.

Steamed Ground-Rice Lotus-leaf Wrapped Chicken in Onion Oil *(for 6–10 people with other dishes for a dinner party)*

 1.6–1.8 kg (3½-4 lbs) chicken
 5 slices root-ginger
 3 cloves garlic
 3 tbs soya sauce
 2 tbs yellow bean paste sauce
 3 tbs hoisin sauce
 1 tbs vegetable oil
 1½ tsp salt
 pepper (to taste)
 150 g (5 oz) coarsely ground rice
 4 stalks spring onion

2 large sheets of lotus leaves
3½ tbs lard

Preparation
Clean the chicken. Boil it for 5 mins and drain. Chop it through the bone into 20 bite-sized pieces and place these in a dish. Cut the ginger up finely, crush and chop the garlic coarsely. Add to the chicken pieces with soya sauce, soya bean paste, hoisin sauce, oil, salt and pepper. Mix and rub all these ingredients into the chicken pieces. Leave the chicken to marinate for 3 hours. Heat the ground rice on a dry wok or pan until it begins to brown. Sprinkle the marinated chicken pieces with the browned ground rice. Mix thoroughly until each piece of the chicken is well coated. Cut the spring onion into 3 cm (1½ in) slices. Soak the lotus leaves in warm water for 10 mins. Drain well.

Cooking
Place the chicken pieces in the centre of double layers of lotus leaves. Wrap them up into a parcel and tie securely with string. Place the parcel in a heatproof dish and cover the top with foil. Place the dish in a deep wok and fill with 900–1.1 litres (1½– 2 pints) of water which should come just half way up the dish. Bring the water to the boil, cover the wok and reduce the heat so that the water simmers. Simmer gently for 2 hours, replenishing the water when necessary.

Serving
Bring the lotus leaf wrapped parcels of chicken to the table. Cut the string with a pair of scissors and unwrap the chicken pieces. Heat the lard in a wok, add salt and spring onion slices. Stir over a medium heat for 1½ mins. Spoon the onion and hot fat evenly over the chicken pieces. This

is a great dish to eat with plain steamed or boiled rice. The browned ground rice imparts a pleasing aroma to the dish.

Duck-and-Chicken Rice with Broccoli and Spring Cabbage
(for 6–8 people to be eaten as a meal on its own)

- ½ duck (about 1.3 kg/2 lb)
- ½ chicken (about 1.3 kg/2 lb)
- 450 g (1 lb) belly pork
- 225 g (½ lb) ham or gammon
- 225 g (½ lb) bamboo shoots
- 450 g (1 lb) broccoli
- 350 g (¾ lb) spring cabbage
- 75 g (3 oz) green mustard pickle ('Snow Pickles')
- 700 g (1½ lb) rice
- 2 tsp salt
- 2 tbs soya sauce

Preparation
Boil the duck, chicken and pork for 10 mins. Drain. Cut the ham or gammon and bamboo shoots into 1 cm (½ in) cubes. Cut the broccoli and cabbage into 3.5 cm (1½ in) slices and coarsely chop the pickle. Boil the rice for 8 mins. Drain.

Cooking
Heat 1.4 litres (2½ pints) of water in a deep wok. Add the duck, chicken and pork. When it comes to the boil again reduce the heat to low and simmer for 1¼ hours. Take out the meat. Cut the pork into 1 cm (½ in) pieces and the duck and chicken meat into roughly 2.5 cm (1 in) cubes. Skim the excess fat off the stock in the wok. Return all the meat to the wok, together with the ham, pickle and bamboo shoots. Bring to the boil and boil for 5 mins before stirring in the parboiled rice. Reduce the heat and simmer the stock, stirring the rice and stock every few

mins. Cook for about 20–25 mins by which time the rice will have absorbed most of the stock.

Meanwhile, heat the lard in another wok. When it has melted, add salt, broccoli and spring cabbage. Stir-fry over a medium heat for 3 mins. Add 4 tbs water and continue cooking and stirring for another 3 mins. Reduce the heat to low and leave to simmer gently for a further 3 mins.

Serving

Pour the rice mixture into a very large deep-sided dish placed at the middle of the table. Spoon the broccoli and cabbage evenly over it.

Arrange at least 3 saucer-sized dishes of dipping sauces surrounding the main dish at the centre of the table. These sauces should contain a mixture of soya sauce, chopped ginger, spring onion, garlic and sesame oil into which the diners should dip their pieces of duck and chicken before putting them into their mouths. This is a homely family type of dish.

Braised Duck with Asparagus, Bamboo Shoots and Mushrooms *(for 4–6 people with 1 or 2 other dishes)*

225–275 g (8–10 oz) breast of duck meat
¾ tsp salt
2 tsp mustard powder
6–8 medium Chinese dried mushrooms
3–4 sticks asparagus
150–175 g (5–6 oz) spring bamboo shoots
1½ tbs 'Snow Pickles' (green mustard pickle)
4 tbs vegetable oil
2 tbs lard
3 tbs light soya sauce
6 tbs good stock
2 tbs dry sherry

2 tsp red bean curd 'cheese' (optional)
½ tsp sesame oil

Preparation
Cut the duck meat into .5 × 7.5 cm (¼ × 3 in) strips. Sprinkle and rub evenly with salt and mustard powder. Soak the mushrooms for 20 mins. Discard the stems and cut the caps into 6–7 strips each. Remove the tougher ends of the asparagus and cut slantwise into 5 cm (2 in) pieces. Cut the bamboo shoots into similar-sized pieces. Coarsely chop the pickles.

Cooking
Heat the oil in a wok. When it is hot stir-fry the duck meat in it for 2 mins and remove. Add the lard to the wok. When it is hot add the mushrooms, bamboo shoots, asparagus and 'Snow Pickles'. Stir-fry them over a high heat for 1½ mins. Add the soya sauce, stock, sherry and bean curd 'cheese'. Stir and turn the ingredients well so that the flavourings are well mixed. Reduce the heat to low, return the duck to the wok and turn everything over together. Stir and turn a few times; cover and leave to cook gently for 8 mins. Sprinkle with sesame oil; turn once more and serve.

Serving
Serve on a deep-sided dish or bowl. A tasty and flavoursome dish where the tenderness of the meat contrasts well with the crunchiness of the bamboo shoots and asparagus.

Hangchow Duck cooked in Master Sauce *(for 4–6 people)*

In China, Master Sauce is made in large quantities and stored for when it is needed.

1.6–2.6 kg (3½–4½ lb) duck
4 tsp salt
4 slices root-ginger

For Master Sauce
3 medium-sized onions
450 g (1 lb) pork spare-ribs
75 g (3 oz) Chinese dried mushrooms
3 tbs sugar
5 tbs soya sauce
5 slices root-ginger
3 tbs yellow bean paste
50 g (2 oz) mixture of star anise, cinnamon bark, dried tangerine peel, cloves and dried fennel
3 tbs sherry or red wine

Preparation
Cut the ginger up finely and rub it well with the salt into the duck. Place in a bowl or casserole dish and put a 1.3–1.5 kg (2–3 lb) weight on top for 48 hours. This reduces the water content of the duck. Rinse off the ginger and salt and blanch the duck in boiling water for 30 secs and drain. Prepare the Master Sauce. Slice the onion and put it with all the ingredients in a wok. Add 2 litres (3½ pints) of water. Bring the water to the boil and simmer gently for 1¾ hours over a very low heat. Strain the liquid. You should have about 900 ml–1 litre (1½–2 pints) left.

Cooking
Place the Master Sauce in a wok, bring it to the boil and add the duck. When it comes to the boil again, reduce the heat to very low and place a heatproof plate on top with an added weight over it to press the duck down under the surface of the sauce. Simmer gently for 1 hour. Turn the heat off and allow the duck to cool in the sauce. When it is

cool lift the duck out, place it on a chopping board and chop through the bone into 20–24 bite-sized pieces.

Serving

Arrange the duck nicely on a deep-sided dish. Keep three-quarters of the sauce for using on another occasion and add the rest of the sauce to the wok with the sherry or red wine. Heat and stir over a high heat until the sauce is reduced to a quarter of its original volume. When it cools pour this sauce over the duck pieces in the dish and serve. This dish is often served with wine.

Soochow Red Soya Duck *(for 6–10 people at a banquet or multi-course party)*

This duck is usually served cold as an hors d'ouevre. It is a favourite summer dish in Soochow.

- 1.6–1.8 kg (3½–4 lb) duck
- 2 tbs sugar
- 1½ tsp salt
- 3½ tbs soya sauce
- 4 pieces star anise
- 6 slices root-ginger
- 1 tbs cinnamon bark
- ¼ tsp cochineal or red colouring
- 1 tbs cornflour (blended in 3 tbs cold water)

Preparation and Cooking

Clean the duck. Remove its head, neck and feet and parboil the bird for 10 mins in boiling water. Drain. Place in a deep wok. Add 1 tbs of sugar, salt, soya sauce, anise, ginger, cinnamon and red colouring. Pour in 1.4 litres (2½ pints) of water and bring to the boil. Cover the wok, turn the heat to very low and leave to simmer very gently for 1½ hours, turning the bird over every 30 mins. Remove the duck from the wok, drain and leave to cool. When cool, chop the bird through the bone into large bite-sized pieces. Skim the excess fat from the liquid in the wok. Strain the sauce. Return the sauce to the wok and boil vigorously to reduce it to less than half its original volume. Thicken by adding the blended cornflour and add the remaining sugar. Stir and cook until the sauce thickens.

Serving

Arrange the pieces of duck nicely on a serving dish. When the rich red sauce cools, pour it over the duck.

FISH AND CRUSTACEANS

Braised Whole Fish with Salted Pickles *(for 4–6 people with 1 or 2 other dishes)*

 3 slices root-ginger
 1 fish (about 700–900 g/1½–2 lb carp, bream, shad, bass, mullet, mackerel, etc.)
 1 tsp salt
 pepper (to taste)
 4–5 tbs vegetable oil
 2 rashers bacon
 75 g (3 oz) 'Snow Pickles' (green mustard pickle)
 3 tbs soya sauce
 4 tbs good stock
 2 tbs wine vinegar

Preparation

Finely chop the ginger. Clean the fish and rub evenly with salt, pepper, 1 tbs oil and chopped ginger. Leave to season for ½ hour. Coarsely chop the bacon and pickle.

Cooking

Heat the oil in a wok. When hot, lift the handle of the wok so that the oil will grease a wider area of the bottom of it. Lay the seasoned fish gently into the hot oil and fry it for 1½ mins on both sides. Lift the fish out with a fish-slice and put aside. Stir-fry the bacon and pickle in the remaining oil over a medium heat for 2½ mins. Add soya sauce, stock and vinegar. Mix the ingredients together for a further ½ min. Return the fish to the wok, baste it with the sauce and cover it with pickle and bacon. Cover the wok and leave the fish to cook gently over a low heat for 4 mins. If you don't have a lid to your wok, cook the fish uncovered for 6–7 mins adding 3 tbs of stock so the sauce doesn't dry out.

Serving

This is another popular family-style dish which is served with rice. The sourness of the pickles in the dish, which gives a slight sharp edge to the general salty-savouriness of the dish, makes it particularly appealing to the Chinese taste.

Braised Whole Fish in Hot Vinegar Sauce (*for 4–6 people with 1 or 2 other dishes*)

In this recipe the fish is treated in the same way as in the previous recipe. However, the sauce is completely different.

This dish is often served in the lakeside restaurants in Hangchow. One of its appealing features is the contrasting flavour between the hot sharpness of the sauce and the sweet freshness of the flesh of the fish.

2 slices root-ginger
1 fish (about 700–900 g/1½–2 lb)
1 tsp salt

pepper (to taste)
5 tbs vegetable oil

For Sauce
3 slices root-ginger
40 g (1½ oz) bamboo shoots
½ sweet red pepper
1 green chilli
2 dried red chillies
2 stalks spring onion
3 tbs soya sauce
3 tbs stock
6 tbs wine vinegar
½ tbs cornflour (blended in 2 tbs cold water)

Preparation
Finely chop the 2 slices of root-ginger. Cut the 3 other slices into matchsticks. Finely chop the bamboo shoots, red pepper, chillies and spring onions. Rub the fish evenly inside and out with salt, pepper, finely chopped ginger and 1 tbs oil, and leave to season for ½ hour.

Cooking
Heat the oil in a wok. Lift the handle so that the oil greases a large area of the wok. Fry the fish gently in the hot oil for 2½ mins on both sides. Remove; drain and set aside. Stir-fry the matchstick pieces of the ginger, bamboo shoots, pepper, chillies and spring onion in the same oil over a medium heat for 1 min. Add soya sauce, stock and half the vinegar. Stir and cook the ingredients for 1 min. Lay the fish in the sauce and cook it for 2 mins on both sides. Remove and transfer the fish to a serving dish. Add the remainder of the vinegar and the blended cornflour to the wok. Stir and cook over a high heat for ¾ min.

Serving
Pour the sauce from the wok along the length of the fish, and garnish with all the chopped vegetables.

Squirrel Fish

This fish gets its name because when it is cooked and served its tail curves up like a squirrel, and when the hot sauce is poured over the super-hot fish freshly taken from the boiling oil, it should 'chatter'. However, in reality there are very few eating places where the fish is cooked and served with such culinary precision. If you can achieve the curling of the tail or the 'chattering' when the sauce is poured on you should be satisfied!

3 slices root-ginger (chopped and minced)
1 whole fish 700–900 g (1½–2 lb) carp, bream, bass, trout, mackerel or mullet
1½ tsp salt
pepper (to taste)
3–4 tbs cornflour
oil for deep fry

For Sauce
2 stalks spring onions
25 g (1 oz) bamboo shoots
2 tbs Chinese 'woodears'
6 medium Chinese dried mushrooms
3 tbs soya sauce
1 tbs sugar
4 tbs good stock
2 tbs sherry
2 tbs wine vinegar
2 tbs lard

Preparation

Finely chop the root-ginger. Clean and scale the fish, and slice it open from head to tail. Using scissors, cut out the middle section of the vertebrae and the bones of the fish. Cut 7–8 deep slashes on one side of the fish, and only 2 on the other. These uneven slashes are what makes the fish curl. Rub the fish thoroughly with salt, pepper, and chopped ginger and coat with cornflour.

Soak the mushrooms and 'woodears' in warm water for 20 mins. Rinse and drain. Slice the mushrooms into thin matchsticks, and the spring onion into 5 cm (2 in) pieces.

Cooking

Heat the oil for deep-frying in a wok. Test if it is hot enough by dropping a crumb into it. If it sizzles when it is dropped in, it is ready. Lower the fish into the oil and fry it for 4 mins at a medium heat. Reduce the heat to low.

Meanwhile, melt the lard in a smaller wok and stir-fry the mushrooms, 'woodears', spring onions and bamboo shoots over a medium heat for 1½ mins. Add soya sauce, sugar, stock, vinegar and sherry and stir over a low heat. At the same time raise the heat under the deep-frying wok to the highest (by this time the fish in the hot oil should have already curled) and deep-fry for 2 mins. During the last minute of frying the fish raise the heat under the sauce and stir.

Serving

Lift the fish out sizzling hot and place it on a very well-heated serving dish. Pour the bubbling sauce quickly over the very hot fish on the serving dish. This should cause a sizzling 'chatter'. The noise should draw the attention of the diners to the dish – reminding them that here is a dish which needs to be eaten quickly whilst it is fresh and crisp.

Garnished Steamed Fillet of Fish *(for 4–6 people with 1 or 2 other dishes)*

3–4 slices root-ginger (chopped)
565–675 g (1¼–1½ lb) fillet of sole, plaice, mullet or rock salmon
1½ tsp salt
pepper (to taste)
3 tbs vegetable oil

For Garnish and Sauce
3 stalks spring onion
2 medium firm tomatoes
2 cloves garlic
4 medium Chinese mushrooms
1 tbs dried shrimps
2½ tbs lard
100 g (¼ lb) minced pork
2 tbs good stock
2½ tbs soya sauce
1 tsp sugar
2 tbs dry sherry

Preparation
Finely chop the ginger. Sprinkle the fish with salt, pepper, chopped ginger and ½ tbs oil. Rub into the fish. Cut the spring onion into 3.5 cm (1½ in) pieces and the tomatoes into quarters. Crush and coarsely chop the garlic. Soak the dried mushrooms and dried shrimps for 20 mins in hot water. Drain the shrimps. Discard the stems of the mushrooms and finely chop the caps.

Cooking
Place the fish on an oval or oblong heatproof dish, and put it into a steamer to steam vigorously for 8–10 mins.

Meanwhile, heat the lard in a wok. When it is hot add the mushrooms, spring onions, garlic, pork and tomatoes. Stir-fry quickly over a high heat for 3 mins. Add the stock, soya sauce, sugar and sherry and continue stir-frying for 1½ mins over a medium heat.

Serving
Take the dish with the fish out of the steamer. Drain any excess water and pour the sauce over the fish, piling the garnish on top. Meanwhile, heat the oil (2½ tbs) in the empty wok; when it is sizzling hot pour it all over the garnish.

The interest of this dish lies in the contrast of the plain, fresh savouriness of the fish with the strong salty savouriness of the sauce and garnish.

Poached Fishballs with Shrimps and Mushrooms *(for 4–6 people with 1 or 2 other dishes)*

450 g (1 lb) white fish
1½ tsp salt
pepper (to taste)
2½ tbs cornflour
1 egg white

For Garnish and Sauce
4–5 small button mushrooms
2 stalks spring onion
3 cloves garlic
2 slices root-ginger
3 tbs vegetable oil
75-100 g (3–4 oz) peeled shrimps
1 tsp salt
2 tbs soya sauce
1½ tbs dry sherry
1 tsp sesame oil

Preparation

Chop and mince the fish. Place in a bowl and add salt, pepper, cornflour and egg white. Beat and mix well. Form the fish paste into small ovals, half the size of eggs. Dip them into a pan of boiling water and poach for 3½ mins. Drain. Cut the mushrooms through their stems into quarters and the spring onions into 2.5 cm (1 in) lengths. Coarsely chop the garlic and root-ginger.

Cooking

Heat the oil in a wok. When it is hot add the garlic, ginger, spring onions and shrimps. Sprinkle with salt, and stir-fry quickly for 1½ mins. Add soya sauce and sherry and mix thoroughly. Add all the fishballs and turn with all the other ingredients for 1 min. Reduce heat to low and continue cooking for another 1½ mins. Sprinkle with sesame oil.

Serving

This dish can either be served in a deep-sided dish or in a bowl. It is excellent eaten with rice.

Yangtze Fish Salad *(for 5–6 people with 1 or 2 other dishes)*

450 g (1 lb) filleted white fish (cod, haddock, sole, turbot, plaice, etc.)
1¼ tsp salt
1 egg
150 g (5 oz) cornflour
3 slices root-ginger
3 sticks celery
3 stalks spring onion
100 g (¼ lb) bean sprouts
600–900 ml (1–1½ pints) vegetable oil
2 tbs light soya sauce
1½ tbs wine vinegar

1 tbs chilli sauce
1 tsp sesame oil

Preparation
Cut the fish into thin slices and cut each of these into triple matchstick-sized strips. Rub with salt, wet with beaten egg, and heavily dust and rub with cornflour. Finely cut the ginger and cut the celery into the same sized strips as the fish. Poach the celery in boiling water for 1½ mins and drain. Cut the spring onion into 5 cm (2 in) pieces. Wash the bean sprouts and drain them thoroughly.

Cooking
Heat the oil in a wok. When a breadcrumb will sizzle when dropped in it is hot enough. Add the fish strips into the hot oil a few at a time. Deep-fry them for 2 mins and drain on absorbent paper.

Serving
Place the celery and bean sprouts as a bed on a large deep-sided dish. Arrange the strips of fish in a layer on top. Sprinkle evenly with ginger and spring onions, soya sauce, vinegar, chilli sauce and sesame oil. Let the diners toss and mix the ingredients together before eating. An excellent dish for a light meal. The contrast in texture between the crunchy vegetables and the crispy fish is interesting.

Fish Fu-Yung *(for 5–6 people with 1 or 2 other dishes)*

350 g (¾ lb) white fish (cod, haddock, sole, plaice etc.)
2 slices root-ginger
1½ tsp salt
pepper (to taste)
4 egg whites
50 g (2 oz) ham

2 stalks spring onion
oil for deep-frying
3 tbs peas
1 tbs light soya sauce
2 tbs good stock
1 tbs vinegar

Preparation
Flake the fish coarsely and chop the ginger finely. In a bowl mix the fish, ginger, salt, pepper and egg whites and beat for 15 secs with a fork. Coarsely chop the ham and spring onions.

Cooking
Heat the oil in a wok. When it reaches the stage where a crumb will sizzle when dropped into it remove it from the heat for ½ min. Return the wok to the heat and stir in the egg white and minced fish mixture, stirring all the time with a wooden chop-stick. Continue to stir over a medium heat for 1½ mins. Strain all except for 2 tbs of oil (reserve the bulk of the oil for reuse), and transfer the fish mixture on to a well-heated serving dish. Stir-fry the ham and peas over a medium heat for ½ min. Add the soya sauce, stock, vinegar and spring onions and stir-fry for a further ½ min.

Serving
Pour the ham, peas, spring onion and sauce on top of the white fish fu-yung mixture in the dish, and serve. The appeal of this dish lies in its pristine whiteness and its savouriness. A dish to be eaten with rice.

MEAT DISHES

Chingkiang Pork and Crab Meat Lion's Head Meatballs
(for 6–8 people with 1 or 2 other dishes)

25 g (1 oz) crab meat coral
1 tbs dried shrimps
75–100 g (3–4 oz) crab meat
2 slices root-ginger (minced)
450 g (1 lb) minced pork
1½ tsp salt
pepper (to taste)
1 egg white
oil for deep-frying
100 g (¼ lb) root of spring green (cabbage)
75 g (3 oz) spring cabbage leaves

For Soup
900 ml (1½ pints) good stock
3 slices root-ginger
1½ tsp salt
1½ tbs light soya sauce
2 tbs dry sherry

Preparation
Chop the crab meat coral up coarsely. Soak the dried shrimps in hot water for 20 mins. Drain and chop finely. Flake the crab meat. Finely chop the ginger. Mix the crab meat, coral, pork, ginger and pepper together and bind with the egg white. Form them into 6–8 large, firm meatballs. Grease with a small amount of oil. Cut the spring cabbage root and leaves into 5 cm (2 in) pieces.

Cooking
Heat the oil in a wok. When a crumb will begin to sizzle when dropped into it, lower 3 meatballs at a time into it and then fry for 2 mins. Remove and drain. Repeat until

all the meatballs have been fried. Then fry the spring green roots for 2 mins and remove.

In another wok, boil up the stock with ginger and salt. Add the spring green roots and the 'meatballs'. Sprinkle with soya sauce and sherry. When it returns to the boil, lower the heat to a gentle simmer. Leave to simmer and cook very gently for 40 mins. Fry the spring green leaves in moderately hot oil for ½–¾ min and place them on top of the meatballs. Cook for a further 5 mins and serve.

Serving

Transfer the meatballs, vegetables and soup into a china soup tureen or large soup bowl and bring to the table. The food should be steaming hot. The appeal of the dish lies in the clarity of the soup, and the great savouriness of the 'meatballs'. For people who prefer spicier foods, the 'meatballs' can be broken up with a chop-stick and dipped into dipping sauces, made from soya sauce, chilli and sesame oil, before eating.

Stir-fried Bean Sprout and Bamboo Shoots with Shredded Pork *(for 4–6 people with 1 or 2 other dishes)*

'Snow Pickles' are a typical flavouring in this area. And this dish is often served in homes in Eastern China.

350 g (¾ lb) lean and fat pork
1 tsp salt
1½ tbs cornflour
½ egg white
50 g (2 oz) 'Snow Pickles' (green mustard pickle)
100 g (¼ lb) bamboo shoots
4 tbs vegetable oil
150 g (5 oz) bean sprouts
pepper (to taste)

2 tbs soya sauce
1 tsp sesame oil

Preparation
Using a sharp knife, shred the pork into matchstick strips. Rub with salt, cornflour and the egg white. Cut the pickle and bamboo shoots into similar-sized strips.

Cooking
Heat the oil in a wok. When it is hot stir-fry the pork in it quickly over a high heat for 2 mins. Add the pickle and bamboo shoots, and continue stir-frying for 2 mins. Add the bean sprouts, salt and pepper, soya sauce and lastly the sesame oil. Stir for 1 min and serve.

Serving
A great advantage of this dish is that it can be prepared and cooked in a very short time.

Sweet and Sour Pork Chops *(for 5–6 people with 1 or 2 other dishes)*

700 g (1½ lb) pork chops (about 4)
1½ tsp salt
pepper (to taste)
3 tbs vegetable oil
3 slices root-ginger
2½ tbs dark soya sauce
1½ tbs hoisin sauce
150 ml (¼ pint) good stock

For Sauce
4 tbs wine vinegar
2 tbs sugar
1½ tbs light soya sauce

2 tbs tomato purée
1½ tbs cornflour (blended in 5 tbs cold water)
2 tbs sherry or white wine

Preparation
Cut each pork chop through the bone into 4 bite-sized pieces. Sprinkle and rub with salt and pepper. Mix the sauce ingredients together in a bowl until well blended.

Cooking
Heat oil and ginger in a wok. When it is hot add the pork chop pieces and stir them in the hot oil until they are slightly brown. Add the soya sauce, hoisin sauce and stock. Bring to a rapid boil. Stir the chops in the bubbling sauce. Leave to cook, covered, for 12–15 mins or until the sauce has been reduced to no more than a tenth of its original volume. Discard the ginger, and turn the contents over a few more times. Pour in the sauce mixture. Continue stirring until the sauce has thickened and become translucent.

Serving
Serve hot with rice. When supplemented with vegetables, this makes a good homely meal. It is often also served in restaurants in China as a change from the normal soya sauce flavoured, deep-fried, or clear simmered dishes.

Quick-fried Diced Ham with Shrimps and Lotus Seeds *(for 4–6 people with 1 or 2 other dishes)*

75 g (3 oz) dried lotus seeds
4 large Chinese dried mushrooms
150 g (5 oz) ham or gammon
50 g (2 oz) bamboo shoots
2 stalks spring onion
2 slices root-ginger

3 tbs vegetable oil
175 g (6 oz) shrimps (fresh or frozen)
1½ tbs soya sauce
1½ tbs dry sherry
1 tsp salt
pepper (to taste)
1 tbs cornflour (blended in 4 tbs cold water)
1 tbs lard

Preparation
Soak the lotus seeds overnight. Drain. Boil in fresh water for 10 mins. Drain. Soak the mushrooms in hot water for 25 mins. Drain. Discard the stems and cut the caps into 8 square pieces. Cut the ham or gammon and bamboo shoots into small cubes. Cut the spring onion into 1 cm (½ in) pieces. Finely chop the ginger.

Cooking
Heat the oil in a wok. When it is hot stir-fry the ginger and mushrooms in it for ¾ min followed by the ham, bamboo shoots, lotus seeds and shrimps. Continue stir-frying over a high heat for 2½ mins. Add the soya sauce and sherry and season to taste with salt and pepper. Stir the mixture around a few times. Pour in the blended cornflour and add the lard. Cook and stir for another min. When the lard has melted the sauce should be glossy.

Serving
Serve on a well-heated dish. A good dish to eat with rice. It goes well with wine.

East China

VEGETABLES

Cauliflower Fu-Yung *(for 4–6 people with 1 or 2 other dishes)*

1 large cauliflower
4–5 egg whites
5 tbs good stock
5 tbs milk
1½ tsp salt
pepper (to taste)
1½ tbs cornflour
50 g (2 oz) ham
3 tbs vegetable oil
1 chicken stock cube (dissolved in 8 tbs water)

Preparation
Break the cauliflower into individual florets (about 5 cm (2 in) each). Cut away the tougher roots. Cut the stem into 3.5 cm (1½ in) pieces. Beat the egg white for 1 min with a pair of chop-sticks or a fork. Add stock, milk, salt, pepper and cornflour and beat together for ½ min. Chop the ham up coarsely.

Cooking
Heat the oil in a wok. When it is hot add the cauliflower stems and stir them in the hot oil for 1 min. Add the florets and continue stirring them together over a medium heat for 1 min. Pour in the dissolved chicken stock cube and cook, covered over a medium heat for 2½–3 mins or until nearly all the stock has evaporated. Stir in the egg mixture and keep on stirring until the sauce has thickened. Reduce the heat to very low and continue cooking and stirring slowly for another min.

Serving
Pour into a deep-sided serving dish. Sprinkle with chopped ham and serve.

Mixed Vegetables with Pea-Starch Transparent Noodles
(for 6–8 people with 1 or 2 other dishes)

- 5–6 medium Chinese dried mushrooms
- 50 g (2 oz) 'woodears'
- 1½ tbs dried shrimps
- 75 g (3 oz) transparent noodles
- 225 g (½ lb) fresh asparagus
- 100 g (¼ lb) bamboo shoots
- 1 medium-sized aubergine
- 225 g (½ lb) broccoli
- 1 chicken stock cube
- 300 ml (½ pint) good stock
- 900 ml (1½ pints) oil for deep-frying
- 100 g (¼ lb) minced pork
- 2 tbs light soya sauce
- 1½ tbs shrimp sauce
- 1 tsp sesame oil

Preparation
Soak the dried mushrooms, 'woodears' and dried shrimps in 600 ml (1 pint) of boiling water for 20 mins. Drain. Discard the stems of the mushrooms and cut the caps into quarters. Soak the noodles in water for 20 mins. Drain and cut into 7.5 cm (3 in) lengths.

Remove the tough roots of the asparagus. Cut slantwise into 5 cm (2 in) pieces. Cut the bamboo shoots and aubergine into similar-sized strips. Break and cut broccoli into 5 cm (2 in) pieces. Crumble and dissolve the stock cube in the stock.

Cooking
Heat the oil in a wok. When a crumb will sizzle when dropped into it stir-fry the aubergines, asparagus, bamboo shoots and broccoli in it for 2 mins. Put to one side. Drain all except 2 tbs of the oil. (The oil can be stored and reused for deep frying.) Stir-fry the pork, shrimps and mushrooms over a high heat for 1½ mins. Add the 'woodears', pour in the stock, soya sauce and shrimp sauce. Bring to the boil and then reduce the heat and simmer gently for 2 mins. Add the once-fried vegetables. Cover the wok and cook gently for a further 3 mins. Add the soaked noodles, raise the heat and stir them around with the ingredients for 1 min. Sprinkle with sesame oil and serve.

Serving
This is a big dish, and is good eaten with large quantities of rice. It is good to serve when there are a lot of mouths to feed.

Quick-fried French Beans with Dried Shrimps *(for 4–6 people with 1 or 2 other dishes)*

450 g (1 lb) French beans
3 cloves garlic
2 tbs dried shrimps
600 ml –1.1 litres (1–2 pints) oil for deep-frying
1½ tbs lard (or butter)
1½ tbs soya sauce
1 tbs shrimp sauce
4 tbs good stock

Preparation
Top and tail the beans, wash and drain. Crush the garlic and chop it coarsely. Soak the shrimps in water for 20 mins and chop coarsely.

Cooking

Heat the oil in a wok. When it is hot enough i.e. when a crumb will sizzle when dropped into it, fry the beans in it over a medium heat for 2 mins. Drain thoroughly. Pour away the oil and store for reuse. Melt the lard in the wok. When it has melted quickly stir-fry the dried shrimps for ¼ min. Add the garlic and continue stir-frying for 1 min. Return the beans to the wok and turn and mix them with the other ingredients over a medium heat for 1 min. Sprinkle evenly with soya sauce, shrimp sauce and stock. Turn the beans in the boiling sauce for 2 mins and serve.

Serving

This vegetable dish is good enough to be eaten alone with plain boiled rice even without a meat dish. Since most Chinese who live in the countryside are largely non-meat eaters, these dishes play an important part in their diet.

Braised Aubergine with Bean Curd Cheese *(for 5–6 people with 1 or 2 other dishes)*

- 3 medium-sized aubergines
- 3 cloves garlic
- 1½ cakes (about 2½ tbs) red bean curd 'cheese'
- 4 tbs good stock
- 600 ml (1 pint) oil for deep-frying
- 2 tbs lard (or butter)
- 1 tbs wine vinegar
- 1½ tbs light soya sauce
- 1 tbs shrimp sauce
- 1 tbs chilli sauce
- 3 tbs red wine

Preparation
Cut the aubergine into small chip-sized strips. Crush and chop the garlic coarsely. Mash the bean-curd 'cheese' with stock until well mixed.

Cooking
Heat the oil in a wok. When it is hot (when a crumb will sizzle when dropped into it) deep-fry the aubergine chips in it for 1½ mins. Drain thoroughly and put aside. Pour away the oil and store for reuse. Melt the lard in the same wok. Add the garlic and stir it around in the fat for ¼ min over a high heat. Put the aubergines back into the wok and stir-fry them with the garlic. Add the bean curd 'cheese' mixture, the vinegar and all the sauces. Stir and turn all the ingredients together. Reduce the heat to low and leave to cook gently for 3½ mins. Sprinkle with red wine. Turn the heat to high and turn the food in the wok over once more. Serve.

Serving
In spite of being a vegetarian dish, this is a very rich dish which goes well with plain boiled rice.

Braised Celery with Two Types of Mushrooms (*for 6 people with 1 or 2 other dishes*)

- 450 g (1 lb) celery
- 225 g (½ lb) firm button mushrooms
- 6 medium-sized Chinese dried mushrooms
- 2 tbs Chinese dried shrimps
- 3 medium tomatoes
- 3 tbs vegetable oil
- 2 tbs lard (or butter)
- 1 cake (about 1½ tbs) Chinese bean curd 'cheese'

4 tbs good stock
1½ tbs light soya sauce
1½ tbs shrimp sauce

Preparation
Clean and cut the celery slantwise into 5 cm (2 in) sections and cut the button mushrooms in half through their stems. Soak the dried mushrooms for 20 mins in hot water. Drain. Discard the stems and cut the caps into quarters. Soak the dried shrimps in hot water for 15 mins. Drain and chop coarsely. Cut the tomatoes into quarters.

Cooking
Heat the oil in a wok. When it is hot stir-fry the dried shrimps and dried mushrooms together for ½ min over a medium heat. Add the lard and the celery. Turn them with the other ingredients until the vegetables are well greased. Add mushrooms, the bean curd 'cheese', the stock, soya sauce and shrimp sauce. Stir and turn the vegetables together with the sauce. Leave to cook gently for 4 mins, turning now and then. Add the tomatoes and turn the vegetables over a few more times. Serve.

Serving
Serve in a deep-sided serving dish. This is another tasty and substantial vegetable dish which should be eaten with large amounts of boiled rice.

Stir-fried Courgettes with Peas, Tomatoes and Mashed Bean Curd (*for 5–6 people with 1 or 2 other dishes*)

350 g (¾ lb) courgettes
4 firm medium-sized tomatoes
2 cakes bean curd (about 225g/½ lb)
6 tbs good stock
½ chicken stock cube

East China

½ cake bean-curd 'cheese' (about 1 tbs)
3 tbs vegetable oil
100 g (¼ lb) peas (fresh or frozen)
2 tbs light soya sauce
1½ tbs lard
1 tbs cornflour (blended in 4 tbs cold water)
1 tsp sesame oil
1 tbs chilli sauce

Preparation
Clean and cut the courgettes slantwise into 2.5 cm (1 in) pieces. Cut the tomatoes into quarters and dice the bean curd. Heat the stock and crumble the stock cube in it. Mix and mash the 'cheese' with the stock.

Cooking
Heat the oil in a wok. Stir-fry the courgettes in the hot oil for 1 min. Add the peas and tomatoes and continue stir-frying for 1 min. Add the tomatoes and bean curd. Pour the 'cheese' and stock mixture evenly over the contents. Bring to the boil and leave to simmer gently for 3 mins. Add the soya sauce. Add the lard and pour in the cornflour mixture. Cook and turn the ingredients over for another 1 min. Sprinkle with sesame oil and chilli sauce, and serve.

Serving
This is a colourful, tasty, and satisfying dish which, like the other vegetable dishes, is nutritious and filling enough to stand on its own as a meal. Serve with plenty of plain boiled rice.

Szechuan and West China

INTRODUCTION

The wealth of West China is contained by a ring of mountains surrounding the Upper Yangtze Basin – the province of Szechuan. No amount of flood water caused by the torrential seasonal rain seems able to wash away all the goodness inherent in the soil as the great river, banked in by deep cliffs and ravines, floods out of the famous Yangtze Gorges on to the lower plains of the Great Lake Regions of the Mid-Yangtze provinces of Hupeh and Huanan. As we winged our way into the province of Szechuan from the ancient capital, Xian, on the central plains of North China (the cradle of Chinese civilization during the millennia before Christ) we seemed to be settling on to a vast embroidered plain made up of limitless miniatures of landscaped gardens: every field seemed to have been tended with infinite care, and every hamlet or small village be surrounded by clumps of picturesque bamboo. Despite the vastness of the area, there was nothing undomesticated about it: it was the 'Big Country' made up almost entirely of a myriad of miniature cultivated rice-fields and market-garden farms. It was quite odd, as there are probably very few territories of the world quite like it. Bigness is usually associated with great sceneries and vast enterprises; here it is associated with everything which is small and domestic. Certainly there is nowhere else where more than 100 million people live in one province!

Because the province has been comparatively peaceful and well run during the past seven or eight years there is now almost a surplus of food, and people are eating well. We ate in numerous well-known eating establishments in Chengdu, the capital, and even attended a practical cookery-school session in Chungking, where some forty young chefs were being trained.

In well-watered basin areas the climate is usually hot and humid in the summer. So it is in Szechuan. It seems that in such climates in most parts of the world the foods eaten are hot and spicy. This was what we were told, and this was what we found. This spiciness is generated by the frequent and extensive use of chilli (both fresh and dried) and a special variety of Szechuan pepper (known as Szechuan fagara), used in conjunction with the three strong-tasting vegetables, ginger, garlic, and onion (or spring onion), and the frequent addition of mustard and sesame, as well as all the dried and pickled ingredients. In the first phase of the cooking the flavours of these ingredients are initially liberated through a short period (1–2 minutes) of frying in a limited amount of hot oil (2–3 tablespoons). It is only after the flavours have been imparted into the oil, and the oil has become 'flavoured oil', that the liberated flavours are expanded further through the addition of stock and wine, which results in the creation of a 'sauce' which albeit nameless, is crucial to the ultimate impact and flavour of the dish. Later additions will create only 'diversionary interests'; the character of the dish is generally determined from the beginning.

Whether the eventual dish is to be 'quick stir-fried', long-steamed, or a 'pudding dish' (many of the 'peasant dishes' of Szechuan are of this category, since over ninety per cent of the population are peasants) the initial cooking procedure is the same: chilli/pepper is stir-fried for a couple of minutes in a small amount of oil together with the strong-tasting vegetables and pickle if required. The resultant 'flavoured oil' is then applied to the meat, fish or

Szechuan and West China

vegetables, or whatever material requires long cooking, and these are then steamed or double-boiled for several hours, or for as long as you like.

According to the official publication of the Szechuan 'People's Press', no more than a quarter of the dishes which appear on a Szechuan table are hot and spicy. The rest consist of vegetables and other food materials which are mostly plain-cooked, with the emphasis on freshness. One of the categories of dishes which we often encountered in Szechuan was the 'boiled-in-the-water' vegetable dish. These are prepared usually by blanching the selected vegetables in boiling water for 1–2 minutes and then straining away all the water, which is in turn replaced by clear chicken broth, in which the vegetables are poached for a couple more minutes. Such clear-cooked vegetables are often found to be excellent counter-foils to strong-tasting and spicy dishes. Nevertheless, with dishes which are plain-cooked and only mildly flavoured, 'dipping sauces' are generally provided in case diners find the food under-spiced or under-flavoured. A common sauce or 'dip' on the Szechuan table is 'red oil'. This is made simply by frying, say, 3 tablespoons each of dried and fresh red chilli-pepper in 6–8 tablespoons of vegetable oil for 1–2 minutes over low heat, and then leaving the mixture to soak in the oil overnight, after which the peppers are strained out. This 'red oil' is very useful on the table for pepping up meat, fish, vegetable or noodle dishes, and can often be used in conjunction with mustard to vary the flavour of the 'hotness' required.

It seems that to the more venturesome Western palates the Western Chinese cuisine of Szechuan is a marked territory, although so far I have not seen the crudest of maps. Since to stroll into any territory, however small, without any map to give us guidance is bound to be something of an adventure, let us take our first steps without further ado.

MEAT

Double-Cooked Pork *(for 4–5 people with 1 or 2 other dishes)*

This Szechuan dish is also popular outside the province. Its success lies in its simplicity.

450 g (1 lb) belly pork
2–3 dried chillies
2 slices root-ginger
2 cloves garlic
1 medium-sized red sweet pepper
2 stalks spring onion
3 tbs vegetable oil
1 tsp salt
1 tbs sugar
1½ tbs lard (or butter)
1½ tbs soya sauce
2 tbs hoisin sauce
1 tbs tomato purée
1 tbs 'red oil'

Preparation
Parboil the pork in boiling water for 20 mins. Drain, and when cool cut into thin slices about 5 × 3.5 cm (2 × ½ in) across the lean and fat. Finely slice the chilli and ginger, and crush and coarsely chop the garlic. Cut the sweet pepper into 1 × 3 cm (½ × 1½ in) strips, and the spring onion into 2.5 cm (1 in) pieces.

Cooking
Heat the oil in a wok. Stir-fry the chillies, ginger and garlic for 1 min. Add the sliced pork, sprinkle with salt, and stir-fry with the other ingredients over a high heat for 2 mins. Add the sugar, lard, soya sauce, hoisin sauce, tomato purée, 'red oil' and sweet pepper. Stir over a high

Szechuan and West China

heat for 2 mins until all the ingredients are well mixed. Garnish with spring onion pieces.

Serving
This is a colourful, green and red, dish with a pronounced sweet and hot flavour. It goes extremely well with rice, and should be supplemented with 1 or 2 vegetable dishes.

Szechuan Dry-Fried Pork-Cubes, Quick-Fried with Chillies and Peppercorns *(for 4 people with 1 or 2 other dishes)*

Dishes, such as this one, in which chillies and Szechuan peppercorns are used together are called 'Kung-Po' dishes. Chicken and prawns can also be cooked this way and peanuts, cashew nuts, or diced sweet peppers can be added. These dishes all have that typical Szechuan hot spicy flavour. It is said that the 'heat' of 'Kung-Po' dishes seems to have a delayed effect. They seem mild to begin with but end up as burning hot.

550 g (1¼ lb) lean pork
1 tsp salt
1 tbs cornflour
1 tbs soya sauce
2 dried chillies
2 fresh chillies
3 slices root-ginger
2 cloves garlic
2 stalks spring onion
½ tbs Szechuan peppercorns
3½ tbs vegetable oil
2 tbs lard
1 tbs yellow bean sauce
2 tsp sugar
1½ tbs wine vinegar
1 tbs cornflour (blended in 3 tbs cold water)

Preparation

Cut pork into small cubes. Rub with salt, cornflour, and soya sauce. Chop the dried and fresh chillies coarsely. Finely chop the ginger, crush and chop the garlic, and cut the spring onions into 2.5 cm (1 in) lengths. Using a pestle and mortar, lightly pound the Szechuan peppercorns.

Cooking

Heat the oil in a wok. When it is hot stir-fry the chillies and peppercorns over a high heat for ½ min. Add the pork and stir-fry for 2 mins. Add the lard, ginger, garlic, yellow bean sauce and sugar. Continue stir-frying for ½ min. Sprinkle on the vinegar. Stir in the spring onions and the blended cornflour and cook, stirring, for a further ½ min over a high heat.

Stir-fried and Braised Bean Curd with Minced Meat and Chinese Dried Mushrooms *(for 4–6 people)*

This dish is popular throughout China, but most popular in Western China. This Western Chinese version is spicier than the one served elsewhere as it has chillies in it.

1 medium-sized onion
5–6 medium-sized Chinese dried mushrooms
2 stalks spring onion
3 cakes bean curd
3 tbs vegetable oil
2 dried red chillies
100 g (¼ lb) minced meat (pork or beef)
½ tsp salt and pepper (to taste)
4–5 tbs good stock
2 tbs soya sauce
1 tbs hoisin sauce (optional)
1 tbs chilli sauce
1½ tbs dry sherry

1½ tbs cornflour (blended in 4 tbs cold water)
1 tsp sesame oil

Preparation
Cut the onion into thin slices and dice coarsely. Soak the mushrooms in hot water for 20 mins. Drain. Discard the stems and chop the caps into small pieces. Finely cut the spring onions and chop the bean curd into pieces half the size of sugar lumps.

Cooking
Heat the oil in a wok. When hot add the chillies, onion and mushrooms and stir-fry them together for 1½ mins. Add the minced meat and stir-fry for 3 mins over a high heat. Add salt, pepper and stock, stirring to mix all the ingredients together. Add bean curd, sprinkle with soya sauce, hoisin sauce, chilli sauce and sherry. Turn and mix all the ingredients. Reduce the heat to low and simmer for 3–4 mins. Mix in the blended cornflour, cook for another min, stirring. Stir and turn the mixture a few more times, adding the sesame oil. When the sauce thickens and becomes translucent the dish is ready to serve.

Serving
Accompany this dish with rice. This dish is popular throughout China, but most popular in Western China. This Western Chinese version is spicier than the one served elsewhere as it has chillies in it.

Quick-fried Shredded Pork with 'Yu Hsiang' Combination of Shredded Ingredients *(for 4–5 people with 1 or 2 other dishes)*

The expression 'Yu Hsiang' is a typical and peculiarly Szechuan culinary term which strictly means ingredients which are normally associated with and used in conjunction with fish. These 3 ingredients are ginger, garlic and spring onion. These are stir-fried together, a touch of vinegar is added and a sprinkling of chopped chilli. When this combination of ingredients is stir-fried together over a high heat it provides a very special aromatic taste which is described as 'Yu Hsiang'.

350 g (¾ lb) lean pork
1½ tsp salt
1 tbs cornflour
3 slices root-ginger
3 cloves garlic
3 dried chillies
3 stalks spring onion
3 tbs 'woodears'
3½ tbs vegetable oil
2 tbs light soya sauce
½ tbs sugar
2 tbs lard
3 tbs peas
1½ tbs wine vinegar
1½ tbs good stock

Preparation
Cut the pork into double-sized matchsticks. Rub with salt and cornflour. Coarsely chop the ginger, garlic and chillies. Cut the spring onion into 1 cm (½ in) lengths. Soak the 'woodears' in warm water for 20 mins and then drain.

Cooking
Heat the oil in a wok. When it is hot stir-fry the pork and chillies over a high heat for 2 mins. Add soya sauce, sugar and 'woodears'. Cook and stir together for 1 min. Add the lard. When it melts, add the ginger, garlic, spring onions, peas, vinegar and the stock. Continue stir-frying over a high heat for 2 mins.

Szechuan and West China

Serving
Like Double Cooked Pork, the Yu Hsiang series of dishes belong in the home-cooking repertoire. They are meant to be eaten with quantities of plain boiled rice.

Sliced Fillet of Fish in 'Yu Hsiang' Combination *(for 4–5 people with 1 or 2 other dishes)*

- 450 g (1 lb) fillet of white fish
- 1½ tsp salt
- 1½ tbs cornflour
- 1 egg white
- 3 slices root-ginger
- 3 dried chillies
- 3 stalks spring onion
- 3 cloves garlic
- 3 tbs 'woodears'
- 3½ tbs vegetable oil
- 1½ tbs lard (or butter)
- 2 tbs soya sauce
- ½ tbs sugar
- 3 tbs good stock
- 2½ tbs wine vinegar

Preparation
Clean and cut the fish into 5 × 3.5 cm (2 × 1½ in) pieces. Rub with salt and cornflour, and wet with the egg white. Finely cut the ginger and chilli and slice the spring onion into 2.5 cm (1 in) lengths. Crush the garlic and chop it coarsely. Soak the 'woodears' in hot water for 20 mins. Drain.

Cooking
Heat the oil in a wok over a medium heat. When it is hot fry the fish slices gently in it for 1½ mins on either side. Remove with a slotted spoon and put aside.

Add the lard to the wok. When it melts, turn the heat to high and add the chillies, ginger, garlic and 'woodears'. Stir them around a few times. Add the soya sauce, sugar and stock. When the sauce boils lay the fish slices into it. Turn them over, and sprinkle with vinegar and add the spring onions. Cook over a high heat for 1 min.

Serving
Transfer to a well-heated serving dish and eat hot with rice. This is one of those dishes where physical heat is an essential part of the flavour of the dish, and, therefore, it is best eaten very soon after it has left the wok.

'Yu Hsiang' Vegetables with Transparent Pea-Starch Noodles *(for 4–5 people with 1 or 2 meat or fish dishes)*

150–175 g (5–6 oz) pea-starch transparent noodles
2–3 sticks asparagus
75 g (3 oz) French beans
2 sticks celery
75 g (3 oz) bamboo shoots
75–100 g (3–4 oz) leeks
100 g (¼ lb) Chinese cabbage
3 cloves garlic
3 slices root-ginger
3 stalks spring onion
4 tbs vegetable oil
1 tsp salt
2 tbs lard (or butter)
4 dried chillies
3 tbs soya sauce
150 ml (¼ pint) good stock
1 chicken stock cube
4 tbs wine vinegar
1 tsp sesame oil

Szechuan and West China

Preparation

Soak the noodles in warm water for 5 mins and drain. Cut the asparagus and French beans into triple-sized matchsticks. Blanche in boiling water for 3 mins and drain. Cut the celery, bamboo shoots, leeks and cabbage into similar sized lengths. Crush and chop the garlic. Coarsely chop the ginger. Cut the spring onions into 2.5 cm (1 in) lengths.

Cooking

Heat the oil in a wok. When it is hot stir-fry the French beans and asparagus in it over a high heat for 1½ mins. Sprinkle them with salt. Add the celery, leeks, bamboo shoots, and the cabbage. Continue stir-frying over a high heat for 2 mins. Add the lard, ginger, garlic and chillies and stir-fry for 1 min. Sprinkle with soya sauce. Crumble in the stock cube and add the stock. Add the noodles. When it heats through and bubbles, sprinkle with vinegar, sesame oil and spring onions. Mix 2–3 times.

Serving

Serve this in a large bowl. Since it is a vegetable dish, it should be complemented with a meat, fish or seafood dish and eaten with rice.

'Yu Hsiang' Aubergine *(for 4–5 people with 1 or 2 other dishes)*

The choice of ingredients and the method of cooking them makes this a typical Szechuan dish. The aubergine can be cooked on its own or with a small amount of minced meat; occasionally it is cooked with finely chopped eel. In this recipe minced meat is cooked with the aubergine.

3 dried chillies
3 cloves garlic
2–3 medium-sized aubergines (about 550 g/1¼ lb)
3 slices root-ginger
3 stalks spring onion
4 tbs vegetable oil
1½ tsp salt
225 g (½ lb) minced pork (or beef)
3 tbs soya sauce
1½ tbs yellow bean sauce
6 tbs good stock
3 tbs vinegar
2 tbs lard (or butter)
1 tsp sesame oil

Preparation
Coarsely chop the chillies and garlic. Slice the aubergines into triple-sized matchstick strips. Finely cut the ginger and slice the spring onions into 1 cm (½ in) lengths.

Cooking
Heat the oil in a wok. When hot add the chillies, salt, and minced meat and stir-fry them over a high heat for 2 mins, stirring all the time. Add the aubergine and stir-fry for 2 mins. Add the ginger, garlic, soya sauce, yellow bean sauce and stock. Turn and mix all the ingredients together. Reduce the heat and cook gently for 5 mins. Add the vinegar, lard and spring onions. Cook for a further 1½ mins. Sprinkle with sesame oil and serve.

Serving
You need to eat large quantities of rice with most Szechuan dishes to absorb their spicy flavour. When cooked with deep-fried shredded eels the crispy strips of fish embedded in the dish give an added textual interest as well as providing a contrast in flavour. This was how I

mostly encountered it on banquet and party tables in Szechuan. However, this basic recipe can be produced more easily.

'Tou-Pan' Bean Paste Sauce

This is a popular and typical Szechuan sauce which can be added to recipes to produce the Szechuan flavour. In China it can be bought but in the West it is not readily available as yet though you occasionally find it in Chinese foodstores and supermarkets. You can cook fish, seafoods, meats and vegetables in it. This is how to make the sauce at home:

- 6 tbs ground salted black beans
- 2 tbs chopped garlic
- 1 tbs finely chopped fresh ginger
- 2 tbs finely chopped onion
- 4 tbs 'red oil'
- 2 tbs dark soya sauce

Mix all the ingredients together.

Szechuan 'Tou-Pan' Fish Steaks *(for 4 people with 1 or 2 other dishes)*

- 3 slices root-ginger
- 2 medium-sized onions
- 4–5 tbs 'Snow Pickles'
- 2 rashers streaky bacon
- 4 tbs vegetable oil
- 450–800 g (1–1½ lb) fish steaks (cod, haddock, halibut, etc.)
- 2 tbs lard
- 1 tsp salt
- 3 tsp sugar

3 tbs 'tou-pan' sauce
6 tbs good stock
2 tbs vinegar

Preparation
Finely chop the ginger. Thinly slice the onions. Coarsely chop the pickle and bacon.

Cooking
Heat the oil in a wok. When it is hot gently fry the fish steaks in it for 2 mins on each side. Remove and set aside. Add the lard, ginger, salt, bacon and onion, and stir-fry for 1¼ mins. Add the sugar, 'tou-pan' sauce, stock and vinegar and stir. Return the fish-steaks to the wok. Bury them under the bacon, onion and pickles, and baste them with the sauce. Cook for 5 mins, turning over a few times.

Serving
Serve in a bowl or deep-sided dish. Another delicious dish to accompany rice.

Quick-fried Prawns in 'Tou-Pan' Sauce *(for 4 people with 1 or 2 other dishes)*

Prawns are considered more of a delicacy than belly pork. Also they can be cooked more quickly. Apart from being eaten with rice, as part of a multi-course meal, they are often also eaten as nibbles with wine.

2 slices root-ginger
75 g (3 oz) bamboo shoots
4 tbs vegetable oil
1 tsp salt
450 g (1 lb) peeled prawns (fresh or frozen)
2 tbs 'tou-pan' sauce
1½ tsp sugar

4 tbs peas
3 tbs good stock
1½ tbs soya sauce
2 tbs red or white wine
1½ tbs lard (or butter)

Preparation
Finely chop the ginger and cube the bamboo shoots.

Cooking
Heat the oil in a wok. When it is hot add the ginger and salt and stir-fry them for ¼ min. Add the prawns and stir-fry them for 1 min. Add the 'tou-pan' sauce, sugar, bamboo shoots, peas, stock, soya sauce, wine, lard and butter. Stir and cook over a high heat for 2 mins.

Serving
If you are serving a regional meal this would make a good starter as it will give the meal that unforgettable Szechuan flavour from the start.

Sliced Pork in 'Tou-Pan' Sauce with Green Peppers *(for 4 people with 1 or 2 dishes)*

550 g (1¼ lb) lean belly pork
3 slices root-ginger
1–2 green peppers
100–125 g (4–5 oz) 'Snow Pickles'
4 tbs vegetable oil
1 tsp salt
2 tbs lard
2 tsp sugar
2¼ tbs 'tou-pan' sauce
4 tbs good stock
3 tbs red wine
1½ tbs wine vinegar
1 tbs 'red oil'

Preparation

Cut the pork across the lean and fat into 6 × 3.5 cm (2½ × 1½ in) slices. Finely cut the ginger, and cut the green peppers into 5 × 2.5 cm (2 × 1 in) pieces. Coarsely chop the pickles.

Cooking

Heat the oil in a wok. When it is hot add the ginger, salt, and pork. Stir-fry them over a high heat for 3 mins. Add the pickle, lard, sugar, 'tou-pan' sauce and stock. Stir and turn the ingredients over a few times. Leave to cook over a slightly reduced heat for 4 mins, add red wine and cook for a further min. Add the green peppers. Sprinkle with vinegar and 'red oil'. Stir and cook for 1¼ mins.

Serving

Another hot, spicy dish which is excellent eaten with quantities of rice.

Lotus Leaf Wrapped Long Steamed Chicken *(for 5–6 people with 1 or 2 vegetable dishes)*

- 1½ tbs Szechuan peppercorns
- 3 slices root-ginger
- 1½ tsp salt
- 4 tbs lard
- 1.6–1.8 kg (3½–4 lb) chicken
- 2½ tbs 'tou-pan' sauce
- 2½ tbs hoisin sauce
- 1 tbs sugar
- 2 tbs soya sauce
- 4 stalks spring onion
- 2 large sheets of lotus leaves

Szechuan and West China

Preparation

Pound the peppercorns lightly in a mortar (or just crush with the back of a cleaver). Coarsely chop the ginger. Heat them together with salt, and lard. Stir over a low heat for 2 mins. Pour them into a heatproof bowl and leave to cool and set. When set rub the mixture evenly over the surface of the chicken, inside and out. Leave to season for ½ hour. Mix the 'tou-pan' sauce together with the hoisin sauce, sugar and soya sauce. Rub this mixture evenly over the chicken. Cut the spring onions into equal length sections and tie each stalk into 2 knots. Stuff them into the chicken cavity. Soak the lotus leaves in warm water for 10 mins to soften them. Use the leaves as you would foil and wrap them tightly around the chicken. Tie with a string into a neat parcel.

Cooking

Fill the wok with 7.5 cm (3 in) of water and place the 'parcel' in a heatproof bowl in it. Bring the water to the boil and cover the wok. Steam the chicken for 2½–3 hours. The water in the wok will need to be replenished at regular intervals.

Serving

Bring the bowl or basin containing the chicken to the table, having poured away any excess water which might have collected in the bowl. The host or hostess opens the 'parcel' in front of the diners. The guests help themselves to bite-sized pieces of chicken by pulling them off the carcass with a pair of chop-sticks. The lotus leaves should not be eaten.

The chicken is sometimes also stuffed with chestnuts or yams and mushrooms, which provide additional goodies for the diners. Lotus Leaf Wrapped Chicken is largely a party dish.

Lotus Leaf Wrapped Ground Rice Pork *(for 4–5 people with 1 or 2 other dishes)*

1.1 kg (2½ lb) belly pork
75 g (3 oz) ground rice (coarsely ground)
3 tsp Szechuan peppercorns
2 slices root-ginger
2 tbs yellow bean paste
1½ tbs dark soya sauce
1½ tbs hoisin sauce
1½ tbs 'tou-pan' sauce
3 tsp sugar
2 sheets dried lotus leaves

Preparation
Cook the pork in half a wokful of boiling water for 15 mins. Drain. When cool cut across the lean and fat parts into 7.5 × 5 cm (3 × 2 in) pieces. Prepare the aromatic rice by stir-frying the ground rice and peppercorns in a dry pan (or wok) until the rice is just turning brown. Chop the ginger coarsely. Blend the bean paste, soya sauce, hoisin sauce, 'tou-pan' sauce and sugar into a thick sauce and rub it thoroughly and evenly into the sliced pork. Sprinkle evenly with ginger, peppercorns and ground rice. Soak the lotus leaves in warm water for 10 mins to soften them. Drain and dry them and wrap the pork pieces in them, making a neat parcel. Secure by tying the parcel together neatly with string.

Cooking
Place the 'parcel' in a deep-sided heatproof dish, basin or bowl, and stand in 6–7.5 cm (2½–3 in) of water in a wok. Bring the water to the boil, reduce the heat and simmer. Cover the wok and steam the pork for 3–3½ hours. At the end of the cooking time the pork should be very tender. The water in the wok will need replenishing at approx-

imately ½ hourly intervals. Pour boiling water down the sides of the wok.

Serving
Pour away any water that has formed in the receptacle in which the pork was cooked and bring it to the table in its dish. When unwrapped the pork should not only be very tender and savoury but because of the ground rice coating also very aromatic. The lotus leaves should not be eaten.

Ma-La

The 'Ma-La' flavour characteristic of Szechuan cooking, is a flavour which combines with the hotness of chillies. It is often achieved by blending sesame paste and peanut butter with 'red oil'. The resultant sauce is usually applied to cold meats, such as cold boiled chicken, or roast duck, or meats which have been sliced or shredded. In the western sense they are really salads. In China they are usually used as starters to a multi-course meal.

Bang Bang Chicken *(a starter to a party meal of at least 2–3 dishes for 6 people)*

½ chicken (about 700–900 g/1½–2 lb)
1 medium/large cucumber
1½ tbs sesame paste
2 tbs peanut butter
1½ tbs vegetable oil
2 tsp sesame oil
1½ tbs light soya sauce
3 tbs good stock
3–4 tbs 'red oil'

Preparation and Cooking
Bring 1.1 litres (2 pints) of water to boil in a wok. Add the

chicken, and simmer it for 20 mins. Turn the heat off and leave the chicken to cool in the water for 2 hours. When it is cold cut it into large triple-sized matchstick strips. Cut the cucumber into similar lengths. Mix and blend the sesame paste, peanut butter, oil, sesame oil, soya sauce and stock into a sauce.

Serving
Arrange the cucumber as a bed on a large serving dish and pile the chicken on top. Pour the blended sauce over them, and lace with 'red oil'.

The ingredients should be tossed at the table before serving.

Szechuan Sliced Beef in 'Ma-La' Sauce *(a starter to a meal with 1 or 2 dishes for 4–5 people)*

700 g (1¼ lb) cold roast beef (or salt beef)
2 tbs peanut butter
1½ tbs sesame paste
3 tsp sesame oil
2 tbs light soya sauce
3 tbs good stock
1 large/medium cucumber
3 tbs 'red oil'
1½ tbs mustard powder (blended with 1½ tbs of water)

Preparation
If salt-beef is used boil it for 10 mins in half a wokful of water, and leave it to cool. When it is cold cut it into 5 × 2.5 cm (2 × 1 in) strips. If you are using cold roast beef cut it in the same way. Mix and blend the peanut butter, sesame paste, sesame oil, soya sauce and stock in a bowl. Cut the cucumber into triple-sized matchstick lengths.

Szechuan and West China

Serving
Arrange the cucumber as a bed on a large serving dish. Pile the sliced beef nicely on top. Pour the blended sauce evenly over them. Lace with 'red oil' and mustard. This also makes a good starter for a festive meal. As in the previous recipe, the salad should be tossed at the table before serving.

Boil-in-the-Water

When I was eating in Szechuan I noticed that there were a number of dishes called 'Boil-in-the-Water' dishes which provided a welcome contrast to the hot spiciness of most other dishes. In spite of being light and bland, these dishes always brought out the natural flavour of the vegetables themselves.

'Boil-in-the-Water' Asparagus with Bean Sprouts *(for 4–5 people with 1 or 2 other dishes)*

    450 g (1 lb) young asparagus tips
    350 g (¾ lb) bean sprouts
    600 ml (1 pint) good chicken stock
    1 tsp salt

Preparation
Remove all the tough root ends from the asparagus and cut the rest slantwise into 7.5 cm (3 in) lengths. Blanche the asparagus for 3 mins and drain. Blanche the bean sprouts in boiling water for ½ min and drain.

Cooking
Heat the chicken stock in the wok. Add the asparagus to it and cook for 3 mins. Add the bean sprouts and continue cooking for 1 min. Sprinkle with salt.

Serving

Transfer to a large bowl or deep-sided dish. Serve together with the other hot-spicy dishes on the table and treat as a part soup and part vegetable dish.

'Boil-in-the-Water' Chinese Cabbage with Shredded Ham
(for 4–5 people with 1 or 2 other dishes)

- 700 g (1½ lb) Chinese cabbage
- 100 g (¼ lb) ham
- 3 slices root-ginger
- 600 ml (1 pint) good chicken stock
- 1½ tsp salt

Preparation

Break the cabbage into individual leaves. Cut the leaves in half lengthwise and cut each half into 3 pieces. Cut the ham into thin matchsticks.

Cooking

Blanche the cabbage with the ginger in half a wokful of boiling water for 1 min. Drain and put into a large bowl or deep-sided dish. Heat the stock in the wok. When it boils pour it over the cabbage.

Serving

Sprinkle the cabbage and soup with salt and shredded ham. The ham is there for its flavour which contrasts with the sweetness of the cabbage. Its colour also provides a striking contrast.

Basic 'Master Sauce'

Szechuan cooking frequently makes use of dried spices, such as anise (star anise, and anise powder), cinnamon bark, dried tangerine peel, peppercorns, and cloves. They

Szechuan and West China

are used in long-cooked (often stewed) dishes. The resulting aromatic sauce flavours the ingredients cooked in it but it is also kept and repeatedly reused by cooking fresh foods in it. This sauce is known as 'Master Sauce'. It can be made by cooking the following ingredients together:

1 medium-sized chicken
700 g (1½ lb) spare-ribs
3 tbs vegetable oil
10 thin slices root-ginger
3 tbs star anise
3 tbs cinnamon bark
1½ tbs cloves
3 tbs dried tangerine peel (broken)
2½ tbs sugar
3 tsp salt
6 tbs soya sauce
4 tbs yellow bean sauce
3 tbs 'tou-pan' sauce
1 tsp mixed five spice powder
300 ml (½ pint) red wine or sherry

Preparation
Quarter the chicken. Cut the ribs into individual ribs.

Cooking
Heat the oil in a wok and when it is hot add the ginger, star anise, cinnamon, cloves and tangerine peel and stir them around for 2 mins. Add 1.75 litres (3 pints) of water, sugar, salt, soya sauce, yellow bean sauce, 'tou-pan' sauce, and five spice powder. Bring to the boil and add the chicken and spare-ribs. Boil for 5 mins, remove any scum and add the wine. Reduce the heat to low and simmer gently for 1¼ hours. By this time the meats will have become very well cooked and can be removed and eaten

as part of a meal. The sauce will have become very strong and pronounced in flavour.

In China, and especially in the western provinces, such as in Szechuan, this sauce is used for cooking game, and offal. In many cases the meat needs only to be cooked for a short while (10–15 mins) in the sauce to acquire that distinctive herbal-aromatic flavour. The meat is often then sliced into smaller pieces, and quickly stir-fried with other ingredients and served as a dish in its own right.

Indeed, almost all meats can be cooked in 'Master Sauce' which will give them a pronounced salty-savoury flavour. Meats cooked in this way will last for several days in a hot climate even without refrigeration. Hard-boiled eggs are the most common dish you find prepared in this manner in China. The Chinese often eat them with soft-rice at breakfast time.

Aromatic and Crispy Duck

This is one of the favourite dishes of the region.

Cooking

Parboil a duck for 15 mins to eliminate any impurities and excess fat. Immerse the duck in 'Master Sauce' and simmer gently for 40–45 mins. Remove and drain. Crisp the duck in one of two ways either by deep-frying for 8–9 mins in hot oil, or by putting it into a very hot oven (240 C/475 F/Gas 9) on a wire-rack for 15 mins. When the duck has been cooked, the meat can easily be cut or scraped off from the bone and eaten wrapped in pancakes, (as in Peking Duck).

Aromatic and Crispy Chicken and Aromatic and Crispy Rabbit can be cooked and prepared in precisely the same manner. However, you will need to parboil them for 8–10 mins, cooking them in the 'Master Sauce' for 30 mins, and deep-fry them in hot oil for 7–9 mins or roast them in a very hot oven for 15 mins. Rabbit or chicken cooked this way can be eaten in the context of a Chinese meal by simply bringing them to the table, chopped into large bite-sized pieces. Eat them with rice and other dishes. Alternatively, they can be eaten as a course on their own, wrapped in pancakes and brushed with plum sauce.

Smoked Duck, Chicken and Beef

Smoked foods are probably popular in Szechuan because they last well in the hot humid climate. Their characteristically strong flavour also makes them popular. They include such prized dishes as Aromatic Camphor-Wood and Tea Smoked Duck, Camphor-Wood and Tea Smoked Chicken, Aromatic Camphor-Wood and Tea Smoked Spare-ribs. Unfortunately these are seldom served in Chinese restaurants abroad.

Smoked meats are almost invariably prepared by first cooking them in the 'Master Sauce' (as described in the previous paragraphs). Drain them and leave to cool. When cold place them on a wire-rack and place in an old disused wok with a small pile of dried tea-leaves, camphor wood barks and twigs at the bottom. Place the wok over a low or medium heat. This will make the tea leaves, and bark and twigs smoke heavily and will bring them to the point of ignition. As soon as the smoke starts to belch, cover the wok firmly with a lid. Turn the heat to the lowest. After about 10 mins of smoking, turn the heat off. Leave the meat in the wok under close cover for at least another 10 mins. After a total of about 20 mins of smoking the meat should be sufficiently smoked. Deep-fry it for 2–3 mins. Serve chopped into neat bite-sized pieces.

This recipe shows the natural progression which often takes place in Chinese cooking, in this case from cooking in the 'Master Sauce', to smoking in a disused wok. Each stage of the cooking leaves an indelible mark on the character of the dishes produced.

Cooking and Flavouring with Szechuan Ja Tsai Pickles

Szechuan Ja Tsai Pickles are one of the main pickles used in Chinese cooking. They are usually available canned, and are large green/reddish lump pieces. Before using, they usually need to be sliced, shredded or coarsely chopped. They are salty and slightly hot in taste, and used frequently in flavouring meats, soups, vegetables, noodles or bean curds, as illustrated in the following recipes.

Quick-fried Shredded Pork with Ja Tsai Pickles & Bean Sprouts (for 3–4 people with 1 or 2 other dishes)

450 g (1 lb) pork (lean and fat)
50–75 g (2–3 oz) Ja Tsai Pickles
1 medium-sized onion
225 g (½ lb) fresh bean sprouts
3½–4 tbs vegetable oil
1½ tbs soya sauce
2 tbs good stock

Preparation
Cut the pork and pickles into double-sized matchsticks. Cut the onion into very thin slices. Wash the bean sprouts and drain them thoroughly.

Cooking
Heat the oil in a wok. When it is hot add the onions and pork and stir-fry them over a high heat for 3 mins. Add the pickles, and continue stir-frying over a high heat for 2 mins. Add the bean sprouts. Sprinkle with soya sauce, and stock. Turn and stir them together for another 1½ mins.

Serving
The 'heat' of the pickles makes this a fairly spicy dish. It should be eaten with large amounts of rice.

Noodle Soup with Shredded Pork and Ja Tsai Pickles *(for 3 portions to be eaten as snacks)*

This is a very popular snack dish all along the Yangtze.

    450 g (1 lb) pork (lean and fat)
    65–75 g (2½–3 oz) Ja Tsai Pickles
    450 g (1 lb) noodles, or spaghetti
    1 chicken stock cube
    1 litre (1¾ pints) good stock
    2 stalks spring onion
    2 tbs light soya sauce
    2 tbs dry sherry
    salt (to taste)
    pepper (to taste)

Preparation
Cut the pork and pickles into double-sized matchsticks. Boil the noodles for 5 mins or the spaghetti for 16 mins and drain. Dissolve the stock cube in the stock. Cut the spring onions into 2.5 cm (1 in) lengths.

Cooking
Heat the oil in a wok. When it is hot stir-fry the pork and pickles together over a high heat for 2½ mins. Add the soya sauce and sherry, and continue stir-frying for another 2½ mins. Boil the stock and adjust the seasoning with salt and pepper. Make sure that the stock cube has completely dissolved.

Serving
Divide the noodles equally between the serving bowls. Pour the hot seasoned stock over the noodles. Top the

noodles in the bowls with the pork and pickles from the wok. Garnish with spring onions.

Hot and Sour Soup *(for 4–5 people)*

100 g (¼ lb) cooked meat (chicken, pork, lamb, beef, etc.)
6 medium Chinese dried mushrooms
1½–2 tbs dried shrimps
3 tbs dried 'woodears'
1 egg
2 stalks spring onion
2 cakes bean curd
40 g (1½ oz) Ja Tsai Pickles
2 tbs vegetable oil
1.1 litres (2 pints) good stock
2 chicken stock cubes

For Sauce
2 tbs cornflour (blended in 5 tbs cold water)
2½ tbs soya sauce
½ tsp freshly ground black pepper
5 tbs wine vinegar

Preparation
Finely chop the cooked meat. Soak the mushrooms and dried shrimps in 300 ml (½ pint) of hot water for 20 mins. Drain. Remove and discard the stems of the mushrooms, and cut each cap into quarters. Reserve the water. Soak the 'woodears' for 15 mins in warm water. Drain. Beat the egg lightly. Cut the spring onions very finely and cut the bean curd into small cubes. Finely chop the pickles. In a bowl, mix all the sauce ingredients well together.

Cooking
Heat the oil in a wok. When it is hot stir-fry the shrimps and mushrooms over a medium heat for 1 min. Add the

meat, 'woodears', pickles, stock and stock cube. Bring to the boil. Reduce the heat and simmer for 7–8 mins. Stir the sauce mixture and pour it into the wok, stirring continually until the soup has thickened. Add the bean curd pieces and pour in the beaten egg in a slow stream into the bubbling soup. After ½ min garnish the top of the soup with the spring onions.

Serving
This is quite a substantial and nourishing soup, which will help bulk out any meal. Because of its substance and spiciness it is particularly useful in the winter.

Dan Dan Noodles *(for 4 people as a snack)*

450 g (1 lb) rice flour noodles
1½ tbs dried shrimps
8 medium Chinese dried mushrooms
65 g (2½ oz) Ja Tsai Pickles
700 ml (1¼ pints) good stock
1 chicken stock cube
3 cloves garlic
4 tbs vegetable oil
350 g (¾ lb) minced pork
2 tbs soya sauce
1½ tbs red oil (or chilli sauce)
salt and pepper (to taste)

Preparation
Boil the noodles for 3 mins. Drain in a collander and rinse them under running water. Soak the shrimps and mushrooms in boiling water for 20 mins. Discard the mushroom stems and roughly chop the caps. Finely chop the shrimps. Coarsely chop the pickles. Heat the stock over a medium heat and dissolve the stock cube in it.

Adjust the seasoning with salt and pepper. Crush and chop the garlic.

Cooking
Heat the vegetable oil in a wok. When it is hot stir-fry the shrimps, mushrooms, garlic and pickles in it for ½ min. Add the pork and continue stir-frying for 3½ mins over a medium heat. Add 150 ml (¼ pint) of the stock. As it comes to the boil again add soya sauce and 'red oil' (or chilli sauce). Leave to simmer for 5 mins. Pour in the remainder of the stock and let the mixture come up to the boil before turning it down to simmer for 1–2 mins.

Serving
Pour a kettleful of boiling water over the noodles in the collander. Drain and divide them equally between the serving bowls. Pour the contents of the wok equally over the noodles. This is a very warming and satisfying snack.

Plain Boiled Bean Curd with Hot Dressing *(for 4 people with 2 other dishes)*

  2 tbs Ja Tsai Pickles
  3 cakes bean curd
  3 tbs peanut butter
  1 tbs sesame oil
  2 tbs vegetable oil

  For Sauce
  3 tbs soya sauce
  2 tbs hoisin sauce
  1 tbs 'red oil' (or chilli sauce)
  2 tbs good stock
  1 tbs wine vinegar

Szechuan and West China

Preparation and Cooking
Finely chop the pickle. Heat the bean curd in half a wokful of water for 5 mins. Drain and cut each piece into quarters. Place spread out on a large serving dish. Blend the peanut butter, sesame oil and vegetable oil in a bowl. In another bowl, blend the soya sauce, hoisin sauce, 'red oil' (or chilli sauce), stock and vinegar.

Serving
Sprinkle the chopped pickle evenly over the bean curd. Drip the two dressing mixtures on to it. Although a simple dish, it is very satisfying and makes a good starter. You can also eat it with rice.

Ma-Po Tou-Fu *(for 4 people with 1 or 2 other dishes)*

Ma-Po Tou-Fu is a popular dish not only with the Chinese but also with the Japanese. It is, simply, stir-fried tou-fu or bean curd with a hot flavoured sauce.

3–4 cakes bean curd
5 medium Chinese dried mushrooms
1½ tbs dried shrimps
3 chillies
3 cloves garlic
2 tbs salted black beans
2 stalks spring onion
4 tbs vegetable oil
150 g (5 oz) minced pork
1½ tbs soya sauce
1 tbs chilli sauce (or 'red oil')
3 tbs good stock
¾ tbs cornflour (blended in 3 tbs cold water)
1½ tsp sesame oil
50 g (2 oz) Ja Tsai Pickles (chopped & minced)

Preparation

Simmer the bean curd in half a wokful of water for 3 mins. Drain. Cut each piece of bean curd into a dozen pieces. Soak the mushrooms and dried shrimps in hot water for 20 mins and drain. Chop the mushroom caps and shrimps coarsely. Coarsely chop the chillies and the garlic. Soak the black beans for 5 mins and drain. Finely cut the spring onions.

Cooking

Heat the oil in a wok. When it is hot add the pickles, black beans, chillies, shrimps and mushrooms. Stir-fry them over a medium heat for 1½ mins. Add the pork and continue stir-frying for 3 mins. Add the garlic, soya sauce, chilli sauce and stock, and stir the mixture. Thicken the sauce by adding the blended cornflour, stirring all the time. Finally, add all the bean curd, raise the heat to high, and stir and turn the mixture over in the wok. When all the ingredients are well mixed, sprinkle with sesame oil and chopped spring onions.

Serving

When Ma-Po Tou-Fu is eaten with plain rice, it gives the palate a melting and burning sensation allied with great savouriness. This makes it the centre point of a meal in spite of being made up of inexpensive ingredients.

Canton and the South East

INTRODUCTION

Of all Chinese people the Cantonese must be the most gastronomically indulgent. Since they consume more seafoods and game-meats than anybody else, they consequently put greater emphasis on the freshness of food than anybody else and insist on having their fish and crustaceans live. On the other hand they also indulge in long-cooked dishes and clear and light soups, as well as crispy dishes, and incorporate a good many features from the other regions of China in their cooking. My mother was brought up in Canton, where her father had a large establishment on the Pearl River, just a few miles down river from the city. I was brought up in Foochow, a seaport some 550 miles up the coast, where we ate a lot of oysters and indulged in cooking with wine-lees (or wine-sediment pastes), and served meals with two or three soups.

As China is currently expanding its economy (agriculturally and industrially) by about ten per cent per annum, in a couple of decades some of these features of Chinese provincial cooking should become better known in the West, which has taken so avidly to Chinese cuisine in recent years. But until then perhaps I could introduce to you some of these South Eastern Chinese dishes, which can be prepared comparatively easily in the wok.

Superior Stock: for Soups

Good stock is crucial for making Chinese soups. Cantonese stock is slightly more refined than those produced elsewhere. In making the stock, apart from boiling poultry carcasses and pork bones (spare-ribs etc.) together, and skimming away any excess fat, and other extraneous matters, the Cantonese also include a ham or bacon bone, and, just before the stock is ready, a quantity of freshly chopped or minced chicken meat will be added for the last 3–4 mins of the cooking time. The stock is then double-filtered through sieves and muslin. This stock is sweeter and fresher tasting than one in which only bones and carcasses have been boiled a long time. Once the Cantonese have prepared their Superior Stock they can make any one of their varieties of soups.

SOUPS

This soup should have a pronounced mushroom flavour. I remember having it on many occasions with my mother at the well known Hsing Ya Cantonese Restaurant on the Nanking Road, Shanghai, in the early 1930s. Its delicious flavour has been unforgettable.

Sliced Chicken and Abalone Soup with Chinese Dried Mushrooms *(for 4 people with 2 other dishes)*

225 g (½ lb) chicken breast meat
salt (to taste)
2½ tsp cornflour
1 egg white
75–100 g (3–4 oz) abalone (dried or canned)
8 large or medium Chinese dried mushrooms
150 ml (¼ pint) vegetable oil
900 ml (1½ pints) good stock
1 stock cube
3 slices root-ginger
1½ tbs light soya sauce

Canton and the South East

1 tbs shrimp sauce
pepper (to taste)

Preparation
Cut chicken meat into 3 × 2.5 cm (1¼ × 1 in) slices. Rub with salt, cornflour and egg white. Cut the abalone into slices the same size as the chicken. Soak the mushrooms in a cupful of hot water for 20 mins. Drain, reserving the liquid. Discard the stems and cut the caps into quarters.

Cooking
Heat the oil in a wok. When it is moderately hot add the chicken pieces, one at a time. Give them a couple of turns in the oil (about ½ min) and remove with a slotted spoon. Pour the oil off and reserve for use another day. Add the stock, stock cube and mushroom water to the wok. Bring to the boil. Add the mushrooms and ginger. Simmer gently for 3–4 mins. Add the soya and shrimp sauces and adjust the seasoning with salt and pepper. Finally, return the chicken and abalone to the wok. Leave to simmer for 1½ mins.

Chicken and Sweetcorn Soup with Crab Meat *(for 4 portions with 1 or 2 other dishes)*

- 100 g (¼ lb) breast of chicken meat
- 2 slices root-ginger
- 50–75 g (2–3 oz) cooked crab meat
- 1½ chicken stock cubes
- 900 ml (1½ pints) Superior Stock
- 2 stalks spring onion
- 150–200 g (5–7 oz) sweetcorn
- salt and pepper (to taste)
- 1½ tbs cornflour (blended in 4 tbs cold water)
- 1 tsp sesame oil

Preparation
Chop and finely mince the chicken and ginger. Flake the crab meat. Dissolve the stock cube in the stock. Finely chop the spring onions.

Cooking
Heat the stock in a wok. When it boils add the chicken meat and ginger, followed by the crab meat and sweetcorn. When it boils reduce the heat and simmer gently for 4 mins. Adjust the seasoning with salt and pepper. Thicken the soup slightly by adding the blended cornflour. Stir and mix for ½ min. Sprinkle with chopped spring onions and sesame oil.

Serving
This is another substantial soup, which adds weight to a family meal. Indeed, it can be a snack in its own right.

Fish and Clam Soup with Oysters (or Mussels) *(for 4–5 people with 1 or 2 other dishes)*

  225 g (½ lb) flaky fish (cod, haddock, turbot, etc.)
  18–24 small clams (fresh or canned) or cockles
  salt and pepper (to taste)
  12 medium oysters or mussels
  1½ cakes bean curd
  3 tbs fresh coriander
  1 egg white
  900 ml (1½ pints) Superior Stock
  4 slices root-ginger
  150 ml (¼ pint) white wine
  1½ tbs cornflour (blended in 6 tbs cold milk)

Preparation
Rub the fish with salt and pepper. Place in a covered heatproof dish and stand it in a wok containing 600 ml (1

pint) of water. Bring the water to the boil and steam for 10 mins. By this time the fish should be cooked, and can be easily flaked. Discard bones and skin. Blanche the oysters or mussels in boiling water for 1½ mins and remove them from their shells. Cut the bean curd into small dice. Chop the fresh coriander. Lightly beat the egg white.

Cooking
Heat the Superior Stock in a wok. Add the ginger, fish, clams and oysters or mussels. Bring to the boil and then simmer for 3 mins. Add the bean curd and wine, adjusting the seasoning with salt and pepper. Allow to come to the boil again and then simmer gently for 2 mins. Stir in the cornflour and milk mixture, and cook stirring for another min. Slowly pour in the beaten egg white and cook, gently, for ½ min. Just before serving, sprinkle with chopped, fresh coriander.

Serving
This is another savoury soup, which is much more filling than the previous recipe.

Crab Meat and Lettuce Leaf Soup *(for 4–5 people with 1 or 2 other dishes)*

2 eggs
3 stalks spring onion
3 medium-sized lettuce leaves
100–150 g (4–5 oz) crab meat
1.1 litres (2 pints) Superior Stock
1½ chicken stock cubes
salt and pepper (to taste)
2 tbs dry sherry
½ tsp sesame oil

Preparation
Beat the eggs lightly with a fork. Coarsely chop the spring onions. Tear the lettuce leaves into small pieces. Flake the crab meat.

Cooking
Heat the stock in a wok. Add the stock cubes, and stir until completely dissolved. Add the crab meat and the lettuce leaves. Adjust the seasoning with salt and pepper. Bring to the boil and simmer gently for 1 min. Sprinkle with sherry, spring onions and sesame oil. Stir once more and serve.

Serving
This is a light soup, and should be served from a large soup bowl or tureen so it can be drunk throughout the meal.

Fishball Soup with Watercress *(for 4 people with 1 or 2 other dishes)*

Fishball soup is one of the most popular and common soups in the South-East Coast of China. This is due partly, I think, to the fact that it can be made from most types of fish.

700 g (1½ lb) fish fillet
1½ tsp salt
pepper (to taste)
1 bunch watercress
3 stalks spring onion
1.1 litres (2 pints) Superior Stock
2 chicken stock cubes
½ tsp sesame oil

Preparation

Prepare the fishballs. Remove all the fish bones, and the bits of skin and membrane and chop and mince the fish. Add 3 tbs of iced water into the minced fish, 1 tbs at a time and blend. After the fish meat has been thoroughly worked on and has become quite smooth, blend in the salt. Place this fish paste in the refrigerator and chill for 1 hour. It should become fairly stiff. Make the fishballs by squeezing half a handful of the fishpaste through your fist straight into a large bowl of iced water. They should be 2.5 cm (1 in) in diameter. Put them into a panful of water and slowly bring it to the boil. Simmer for just 1 min. Turn the heat off and leave the fishballs in the hot water for another 10 mins. Remove with a slotted spoon. Clean the watercress thoroughly, removing the roots, and cutting it into 2.5 cm (1 in) sprigs. Cut the spring onions up finely.

Cooking

Heat the stock in a wok and dissolve the stock cubes in it. Add the poached fishballs. Bring to the boil and simmer gently for 5 mins. Add the watercress. Adjust the seasoning with salt and pepper. Garnish with spring onions and sprinkle on the sesame oil.

Serving

This amount of fish should make 20 fishballs i.e. 5 per person. As it is a light and clear soup which has been freshened with watercress and spring onions, it can be drunk and eaten throughout the meal, but keep it hot throughout. The fishballs themselves can be eaten during the meal dipped in a dipping sauce made from soya sauce, vinegar and 'red oil'.

Wontun Soup *(for 4 people with 1 or 2 other dishes)*

Wontun Soup is one of the most popular soups in Canton. Wontun is a type of thin-skinned ravioli. It is made by pressing and wrapping a small amount of meat folded inside a large piece of dough or 'skin'. These days few people actually make these 'skins' themselves, as they can quite easily be purchased from most Chinese food stores. Usually no more than ½–¾ tsp of filling is wrapped in the 'skin', and in Canton these fillings are often made from chopped pork or chicken mixed with chopped shrimps. This soup is served in tea-houses of South China in conjunction with an array of Dim Sums or Chinese light snacks.

20 wontun 'skins'
900 ml (1½ pints) Superior Stock
75–100 g (3–4 oz) fresh shrimps, shrimp heads and tails
3 slices root-ginger
1½ cubes chicken stock
1 bunch watercress

For Filling
5 tbs fresh shrimps
40 g (1½ oz) lean and fat minced pork
2 tsp diced shrimps
½ tsp salt
1 tsp finely chopped ginger
1 tsp finely chopped onion
dash pepper
½ egg white

Preparation and Cooking
Boil the Superior Stock with the fresh shrimps, shrimp heads and tails and the root-ginger for 8–9 mins. Strain. Dissolve the stock cubes in the stock.

Canton and the South East

Make the wontun filling. Soak the dried shrimps in hot water for 20 mins. Drain and finely chop. Mix all the filling ingredients together and fold about ¾ of a tsp of the mixture into each 'skin'. Simmer in the stock for 2 mins. Add the watercress to the stock and simmer another 2 mins.

Serving
Like Fishball Soup, Wontun Soup is a clear soup which can be served and drunk throughout the meal. The important thing is that it should be served hot and the wontuns may be picked out with a pair of chop-sticks and dipped into 1 or 2 dipping sauces, made from soya sauce, chilli sauce, vinegar, or a mixture of these, and eaten.

Leek and Frogs' Legs Soup *(for 4 people with 1 or 2 other dishes)*

8–12 frogs' legs
salt and pepper (to taste)
2 tbs oil (optional)
350 g (¾ lb) young leeks
1.1 litres (2 pints) Superior Stock
1 chicken stock cube
3 slices root-ginger
1½ tbs soya sauce
½ tsp sesame oil

Preparation
Clean the frogs' legs and rub them with salt and pepper. Leave to season for 1 hour. Poach or fry the frogs' legs in hot oil for 2 mins, or until slightly brown, and drain. Wash the leeks well and cut them slantwise into 5 cm (2 in) lengths. Blanche them in boiling water for 1 min and drain.

Cooking

Heat the stock in a wok. Dissolve the stock cube in it. Add the ginger, frogs' legs and leeks. Bring to a gentle boil and continue simmering for a further 4–5 mins. Adjust the seasoning with salt and pepper. Add soya sauce and sprinkle with sesame oil.

Serving

Frogs' legs are extraordinarily similar to chicken in flavour but are considered more refined. When we dined in banquet style at the famous Pang Xi restaurant in Canton, this dish was served steamed in an excavated marrow bowl with Chinese dried mushrooms, straw-mushrooms, bamboo shoots, lotus nuts and sharks' fins. Since sharks' fins need to be soaked for a day, simmered in 3 changes of stock and are very expensive, it is only worth it if there is an unusual amount of time and money available. Otherwise you might try varying the recipe a little. Add in 50 g (2 oz) of transparent pea starch noodles, excavate a marrow and steam the frogs' leg mixture in it for ½ hour.

West Lake Minced Beef Soup with Watercress *(for 4 people with 1 or 2 other dishes)*

This soup is frequently served in Cantonese restaurants, probably because it is quick and easy to make.

- 2 tbs cornflour
- 1 egg white
- 1 tsp salt
- 1½ tbs soya sauce
- 225 g (½ lb) minced beef
- 1 bunch of watercress
- 2 slices root-ginger
- 1 beef stock cube
- 2 tbs vegetable oil

Canton and the South East

1.1 litres (2 pints) good stock (or Superior Stock)
salt and pepper (to taste)
1½ tbs light soya sauce
1 tsp sesame oil

Preparation
Mix 1 tbs cornflour, ½ the egg white, salt and soya sauce into the beef. Leave to season for ½ hour. Blend remaining cornflour with 3 tbs water. Clean the watercress, remove the roots, and cut into 2.5 cm (1 in) sprigs. Finely chop the ginger. Dissolve the stock cube in the stock.

Cooking
Heat the oil in the wok. When it is hot stir-fry the seasoned minced beef and ginger in it until it is well cooked through and broken up rather than stuck together in lumpy pieces. This takes about 2 mins. Pour in the stock. Continue stirring and bring to the boil. Adjust the seasoning with salt and pepper. Add the blended cornflour. Beat the remaining egg white and add it slowly into the soup, stirring continuously. Cook for 1 min. Add the watercress and soya sauce and stir them in. Sprinkle with sesame oil.

Serving
The soup is quite filling and well balanced, having both meat and vegetables in it. If there is no substantial meat or fish dish in the meal, it can be poured on to rice like gravy.

Congee or Soft Rice

In Canton and most of the southern provinces of China, congee or soft rice is frequently served as a snack, especially late at night. The best congee is made by boiling rice with glutinous or pudding rice in six times the usual amount of water. Here is a recipe for it for 4–6 portions.

175 g (6 oz) rice
50 g (2 oz) glutinous or pudding rice

Cooking
Put the 2 rices in a pan with 2 litres (3½ pints) of water. Bring to the boil and then simmer gently for about 1 hour. When cooked it should have the consistency of a light watery porridge.

Gold and Silver or Chicken and Duck Congee *(for 4–5 portions as a light snack)*

100 g (¼ lb) boiled chicken meat
100 g (¼ lb) roast duck meat
2 stalks spring onion
3 slices root-ginger
1.1–1.4 litres (2–2½ pints) congee
2 chicken stock cubes
2 tbs light soya sauce

Preparation
Chop the meats and spring onions up finely. Cut the ginger into fine shreds.

Cooking
Heat the congee in a wok. Crumble the stock cubes and dissolve them in the congee. Add the ginger and half the chicken and duck meats. Simmer gently for 7–8 mins.

Serving.
Serve into 4–5 bowls. Place the remaining meats on top of the rice. Garnish with spring onions and sprinkle with soya sauce. A very warming and settling snack to take late in the evening. Often served towards the end of a mah-jongg party.

Fish and Seafood Congee *(a snack for 4–5 people)*

125–150 g (4–5 oz) fillet of fish
salt and pepper (to taste)
½ egg white
2 stalks spring onion
1.4 litres (2½ pints) congee
4 slices root-ginger
4 tbs peeled prawns (fresh or frozen)
50–75 g (2–3 oz) cooked crab meat
50–75 g (2–3 oz) oyster (meat) or mussels
1½ chicken stock cube
½ tsp salt
2 tbs soya sauce
1 tsp sesame oil

Preparation
Cut the fish into slivers. Rub with salt, and egg white. Finely cut up the spring onions.

Cooking
Heat the congee in a wok. When it boils add the ginger and fish. When it comes to the boil again add prawns, crab meat, mussels or oysters and crumbled stock cubes. Stir and bring to the boil again. Leave to simmer gently for 3 mins. Season to taste with salt and pepper.

Serving
Serve into 4–5 serving or soup bowls. Garnish with spring onion shavings, soya sauce and sesame oil. This is another very warming and settling snack to be eaten late in the evening. It also makes a good light meal during the day.

Cha Siu Barbecued and Roast Meats

The Cantonese are fond of meat and poultry which has a super-crispy skin. They like the meat to be marinaded and then barbecued or quickly roasted at a high temperature so that dried encrustations of marinade can be eaten together with rare meat. Here are some recipes:

Marinated Barbecued Pork *(for 4–5 portions with a soup and a vegetable dish)*

   700 g (1½ lb) fillet of pork
   2 slices root-ginger
   1½ tsp salt
   1 tbs sugar
   1 tbs yellow bean sauce
   1½ tbs dark soya sauce
   1 tbs hoisin sauce
   1 tbs red bean-curd cheese
   900–1.1 litres (1½–2 pints) vegetable oil for deep-frying
   3 tbs golden syrup
   2 tbs dry sherry

Preparation
Trim the pork but retain its natural shape and cut into circular pieces about 4.5 × 6 cm (1¾ × 2½ in) in diameter. Finely chop the ginger. Rub the pieces of meat thoroughly with salt, sugar and the chopped ginger. Leave to season for 1 hour. Thoroughly mix the yellow bean sauce, soya sauce, hoisin sauce and bean curd cheese in a large bowl. Put the pork pieces into this marinade and rub thoroughly with it. Leave them to marinade for at least 1 hour.

Cooking
Heat the oil in a wok. When a crumb will sizzle when dropped into it, add the pork pieces one by one. Turn them over gently, and deep-fry over a medium heat for 6–7 mins. Remove and drain and place on a chopping board. Pour away all the oil (retaining it for other uses).

Meanwhile, pour the remnants of the marinade into the wok. Add the syrup and sherry, and 4 tbs water. Bring to the boil and cook, stirring for 1 min.

Serving
Cut the pork strips across the grain into 5 mm (¼ in) thick disc-shaped pieces. Arrange them neatly in a tile pattern down the middle of a serving dish, or arrange them radiating out from the centre of the dish. Pour the syrupy sauce from the wok over them. The distinction of the pork cooked in this way is that each piece of sliced meat has a rim of near-burnt marinade with a ring of well-cooked meat surrounding a centre of meat which is comparatively rare. This meaty richness is complemented by a sweet sauce. Lamb and fillet of beef can also be cooked in this way. However, beef will only need to be fried for 4–5 mins.

Sweet and Sour Pork *(for 4 people with 1 or 2 other dishes)*

700 g (1½ lb) lean belly of pork
2 tbs cornflour
½ egg
1½ tsp salt
2 slices canned pineapple
1 green pepper
900 ml (1½ pints) vegetable oil for deep frying

For Sauce
1½ tbs cornflour (blended in 4 tbs cold water)
3 tbs wine vinegar
1½ tbs tomato purée
2½ tbs syrup (from canned pineapple)
2 tbs sugar
2 tbs orange juice
1½ tbs light soya sauce

Preparation

Cube the pork, cutting the lean and fat into 3.5 cm (1½ in) pieces. Mix the cornflour with the egg into a batter, season with salt. Coat the pork with the batter. Cut the pineapple and pepper into 3.5 cm (1½ in) pieces. Mix all the sauce ingredients together until well blended.

Cooking

Heat the oil in a wok. When a crumb will sizzle when dropped into it, add the pork pieces, one by one. Stir them around and fry over a medium heat for 4–5 mins. Remove with a slotted spoon and put aside to drain.

Pour away all the oil from the wok (you can store and reuse it) and add the pepper and pineapple pieces. Stir them around a few times over medium heat. Pour in the sauce mixture. Continue stirring until the sauce thickens. Return the pork to the pan and mix it in with the other ingredients for 1 min.

Serving

Sweet and Sour Pork is, perhaps, the most popular Chinese dish in the West. Its appeal probably lies in the contrast of the richness of the pork with the fruitiness of the sauce; a combination which only occurs rarely in western cuisine. Sweet and sour sauce can be applied to most foods, including fish.

Sweet and Sour Fish Steaks *(for 4 people with 1 or 2 other dishes)*

  700 g (1½ lb) fillet of fish (haddock, cod, halibut, etc.)
  2 tbs cornflour
  1 egg
  2½ tsp salt, and pepper (to taste)
  1 slice pineapple

1 green pepper
600 ml (1 pint) vegetable oil for deep-frying

For Sauce
Same as in the previous recipe.

Preparation
Cut the fish into 8.5 cm (2½ in) chunks. Mix the cornflour and egg into a batter. Rub the fish with salt and pepper and coat in the batter. Cut the pineapple into 2.5 cm (1 in) pieces. Prepare the sauce mixture as in the previous recipe.

Cooking
Heat the oil in a wok. When a crumb will sizzle when dropped into it, add the fish pieces one by one. Fry the fish for 2½ mins and remove with a slotted spoon. Drain. Pour away the oil from the wok (you can store it for reuse). Add the ginger, pineapple and pepper and stir them around a few times. Pour in the sauce mixture and continue stirring until the sauce thickens. Return the fish pieces to the wok. Mix all the ingredients together. Cook gently for 1½ mins.

Serving
This dish should be eaten with rice. The appeal of the dish lies partly in the contrast between the sauce, and the flavour of the fish, which is somewhat more heavily seasoned than the pork in the previous recipe. This is a good way to serve fish, if the meat dish served with it is soya-braised or hot-cooked in the Szechuan style.

Sweet and Sour Prawns *(for 4 people with 1 or 2 meat and vegetable dishes)*

Prawns are one of the quickest foods to stir-fry. They usually do not take much more than 1½ mins; although large frozen prawns often need to be cut up before cooking.

Otherwise, you only need to prepare the sauce, which is much the same as in the two previous recipes.

>700 g (1½ lb) large prawns
>1½ tsp salt
>1½ tbs cornflour
>2 slices root-ginger
>1 slice pineapple
>1 green pepper
>4–5 tbs vegetable oil

For Sauce
Same ingredients as in the previous 2 recipes.

Preparation
Shell, devein and thoroughly rinse the prawns. Rub with salt and cornflour. Finely chop the ginger and cut the pineapple and pepper into approximately 2.5 cm (1 in) pieces. Prepare the sauce as in the previous 2 recipes.

Cooking
Heat the oil in a wok. When it is hot add the ginger and stir it around a few times, then add the prawns. Continue stir-frying over a high heat for 1½ mins. Remove with a slotted spoon.

Add the pineapple and pepper and stir them around a few times. Pour in the sauce mixture. Stir until the sauce becomes clear and translucent. Return the prawns to the wok. Continue to stir-fry gently for ¾ min.

Serving
Serve on a well-heated serving dish and eat immediately with rice and a vegetable or meat dish, or both.

Crispy Skin Meat Dishes

The Cantonese love crispy skinned meat. The classic example is suckling pig, which is barbecued and cooked until the skin is entirely crispy and is carved off first to be eaten on its own. It is also served in small steamed buns or pancakes (in the same manner as the skin of Peking Duck is often eaten). However, as suckling pigs are not readily available and are too much for any ordinary domestic situation, we shall concentrate only on meats which can be cooked in smaller quantities.

Crispy Skinned Pork *(for 4–5 people with rice and 1 or 2 vegetable dishes)*

- 1.5–1.6 kg (3–3½ lb) shoulder or belly pork
- 3 tsp salt
- 2 tbs cornflour
- ½ tsp five spice powder (optional)
- 1½ tbs soya sauce
- 1½ tbs hoisin sauce
- 2 tsp honey
- 600 ml (1 pint) vegetable oil

Preparation
Clean and rub the pork skin thoroughly with salt, cornflour and five spice powder. Leave to season for 3 hours. Heat 1.1 litres (2 pints) of water in a wok. When it boils lower the pork, skin side down, into it and boil for 20 mins. Remove and drain thoroughly. When dry rub the skin with soya sauce, hoisin sauce and honey. Leave to season for 15 mins.

Cooking
Heat the oil in a wok. When a crumb will sizzle when dropped into it, lower the pork skin side down into it. Fry over a low/medium heat for 10–11 mins. Remove and drain.

Serving

The skin should now be quite crispy. Cut the pork through the skin into 5 cm (2 in) triangular, rectangular or diamond-shaped pieces, each with a piece of skin attached. The crispy skin is good eaten with plain rice, or inserted into steamed buns or pancakes and eaten doused with hoisin sauce. It can also be sprinkled with a mixture of salt and five spice powder. Use the proportion of 10 times as much salt as spice powder and heat them together in a dry pan or wok for 1 min. This should make them more aromatic.

Deep-fried Crispy Chicken *(for 4–5 people with rice and 1 or 2 vegetable dishes)*

1 young chicken (1.4–1.8 kg/3–4 lb)
3 tsp salt
1½ tbs dry sherry
2 tbs soya sauce
2 tbs hoisin sauce
1½ tbs cornflour
3 slices root-ginger
3 stalks spring onion
1.1 litres (2 pints) oil for deep-frying

For Dip
2 tbs salt
1½ tsp five spice powder

Preparation

Rub the chicken skin with salt and sherry and hang the bird up to dry for 4–5 hours. Boil in a wok or pan for 15 mins and drain thoroughly. When dry rub all over with soya sauce, hoisin sauce and cornflour. Finely chop the ginger and cut the spring onion into 7.5 cm (3 in) lengths and stuff them into the cavity of the chicken.

Cooking
Heat the oil in the wok. When it is hot lower the chicken into it and fry over a low/medium heat, turning it around regularly, for 12–15 mins until golden brown. Remove and drain.

Heat the salt and five spice powder in a dry pan for 1 min.

Serving
Place the chicken on a chopping board and chop into large bite-sized pieces. Sprinkle evenly with the salt and five spice mixture. The skin of the chicken should be both spicy and crispy. It is good with plain rice and vegetables.

Crispy and Spicy Chicken Liver and Gizzards *(for 4 people with rice and 1 or 2 vegetable dishes)*

350 g (¾ lb) chicken gizzards
350 g (¾ lb) chicken livers
2 tbs cornflour
2 stalks spring onion
2 slices root-ginger
300 ml (½ pint) vegetable oil
½ tsp freshly ground pepper

For Marinade
1 tbs dry sherry
2 tbs soya sauce
1½ tsp salt
2 tsp sugar

Preparation
Remove the fat and outer membranes of the gizzards. Trim and cut each liver and gizzard into 2. Wash and drain. Mix all the marinade ingredients together and pour over the liver and gizzards. Leave for 1 hour. Pour away

the marinade and dredge the liver and gizzards in cornflour. Finely chop the spring onions and ginger.

Cooking

Heat the oil in a wok. When a crumb will sizzle when dropped into it add the marinaded liver and gizzards in 4 batches. Using a slotted spoon, turn the gizzards and liver in the hot oil while you cook them over a medium heat for 3½ mins. Remove and drain.

Serving

Serve on a very dry well-heated dish. Sprinkle evenly with pepper and spring onions. Because of the spiciness of this dish it goes well with plain rice and 1–2 accompanying dishes (one should be a vegetable). It can also be served as a starter or as a nibble with wine.

Dishes Using Black Bean Sauce

Salted black beans are used extensively as a flavouring ingredient in South East China. Besides being inexpensive they can be used to flavour almost any meat, poultry, fish and seafood dishes. They can be used in a variety of ways. They can be soaked in water for 5–6 minutes and drained before being incorporated in a dish, or simply finely chopped and stir-fried in a small amount of oil for 1-2 mins (this releases the flavour), together with some strong-tasting vegetables, such as chopped garlic, ginger, and onion. Chopped dried or fresh chillies are sometimes also added to make the beans spicy. A few tablespoons of good stock and wine are then added to enlarge the flavoured oil into a sauce. Most stir-fried foods can then be turned in the sauce to take on a coating of its distinctive flavour.

Canton and the South East

Black bean sauce carries an earthy savouriness, which is easily acceptable to most palates. Meats and seafoods cooked in the sauce are often tossed with noodles or other bulk-foods to provide a more substantial dish.

Quick-Fried Chicken in Black Bean Sauce *(for 4 people with 1 or 2 other dishes)*
This is a favourite Cantonese snack.

- 450 g (1 lb) breast of chicken
- 1 tsp salt
- 1½ tbs cornflour
- 1½ tbs salted black beans
- 3 slices root-ginger
- 2–3 cloves garlic
- 1 medium-sized onion
- 2 chillies
- 1 green pepper
- 6 tbs vegetable oil
- 3 tbs good stock
- 1½ tbs soya sauce
- 1 tbs wine vinegar

Preparation
Cut the chicken meat into small cubes. Rub them with salt and dredge them with cornflour. Finely chop the black beans, ginger, garlic, onion and chillies. Cut the green pepper into 2.5 cm (1 in) pieces.

Cooking
Heat the oil in a wok. When it is hot add the chicken pieces and stir and turn them in the oil over a high heat for 2 mins. Remove with a slotted spoon and drain. Pour away all but 1½ tbs of the oil. Add the black beans, ginger, garlic, onion and chillies. Stir-fry them in the oil over a medium heat for ¾ min. Add the stock, soya

sauce, vinegar and green pepper. Bring to the boil and cook for 1 min. Return the once-fried chicken pieces to the wok. Stir them with the sauce and other ingredients over a high heat for 1½ mins and serve.

Serving
The chicken in the dish has by now quite a spicy coating of sauce, which carries with it a very pronounced and individual savouriness. Because of the comparatively short period of time the chicken is subjected to high-heat cooking much of the natural juices in the chicken will be retained.

In China this dish is cooked with the chicken on the bone. It will, initially, be stir-fried over a high heat for at least 3–4 mins before being drained. When serving, the chicken will be chopped through the bone into large bite-sized pieces.

Stir-fried Sliced Beef in Black Bean Sauce with Noodles
(for 4 people to be eaten as a snack)

450 g (1 lb) beef steak (fillet, rump, sirloin, topside)
1½ tsp salt
1½ tbs cornflour
½ egg white
450 g (1 lb) rice-flour noodles
6 tbs vegetable oil

For Sauce
1½ tbs salted black beans
3 slices root-ginger
3 cloves garlic
2 medium-sized onions
3 green chillies
1 medium-sized red pepper
1 medium-sized green pepper
6 tbs good stock

2 tbs soya sauce
2 tbs dry sherry
1 tbs wine vinegar

Preparation
Cut the beef into very thin strips 5 × 2.5 cm (2 × 1 in). Rub with salt and cornflour and wet with egg white. Boil the noodles for 4 mins, and drain. Rinse under cold water to separate them. Finely chop the black beans, ginger, garlic, onions and chillies. Cut the sweet pepper into 1 × 2.5 cm (½ × 1 in) pieces.

Cooking
Heat the oil in a wok. When it is hot, add the beef strips and spread them evenly over the wok. Stir-fry them quickly for 1 min and remove with a slotted spoon. Stir-fry all the solid ingredients of the sauce over a high heat for 1 min. (This releases their flavours.) Add the sweet peppers and pour in half the stock, 1 tbs soya sauce, 1 tbs sherry and vinegar. Stir over a high heat for 1 min.

Return the beef to the wok and mix in with all the other ingredients. Remove two-thirds of the mixture and add the noodles to the rest. Heat and mix the noodles in well.

Serving
Transfer the coated noodles in the wok to a large serving dish. Return the remaining mixture to the wok. Boil it up briefly and add the rest of the stock and the remaining soya sauce and sherry. Pour this mixture over the noodles as a type of garnish.

Quick-fried Scallops and Prawns with Black Bean Sauce
(for 4 people with 1 or 2 other dishes)

12 large prawns (fresh or frozen)
8 medium or large scallops

2½ tsp salt
1½ tbs cornflour
1 egg white
175–225 g (6–8 oz) can miniature corn
1 medium-sized onion
3 tbs vegetable oil
4 tbs peas

For Sauce
1½ tbs salted black beans
3 slices root-ginger
2 cloves garlic
2 stalks spring onion
2 tbs good stock
1½ tbs dry sherry
1 tbs soya sauce

Preparation
Clean, shell and devein the prawns. Remove the meat and coral from the scallops. Rub them with salt, dredge with cornflour and wet with egg white. Cut each corn slantwise in half and the onion into thin slices. Finely chop the black beans, ginger, garlic and spring onions.

Cooking
Heat the oil in a wok and stir-fry the onion in it for ½ min. Add the scallops and prawns and stir-fry them for 1 min. Add the corn and continue stir-frying for 1 more min. Remove and drain.

Add the solid ingredients of the sauce to the remaining oil in the wok. Raise the heat and stir-fry them over a high heat for ¾ min. Add stock, sherry and soya sauce. Stir a few times. Return the scallops, prawns and corn to the wok. Add the peas and cook, stirring, for 1 min.

Canton and the South East

Serving
This is an exceptionally tasty and flavoursome dish, which is excellent eaten with rice. It is also good on its own as a nibble with wine. It is a dish which is often served in restaurants since it is so quick and easy to prepare.

Fukien Crab Rice with Leeks and Black Bean Sauce *(for 4–5 people, to be eaten as a big snack)*

Although this is a rough coastal dish there are few things in the culinary world to beat it for seafood savouriness. In Fukien along the South-east coast 'wine sediment paste' (made from wine lees) is added to the sauce. Here we are substituting brandy and tomato purée.

3–4 medium crabs (weighing 450 g/1 lb each)
700 g (1½ lb) leeks
4–5 slices root-ginger
150 g (5 oz) glutinous rice or pudding rice
6 tbs vegetable oil
2 tsp salt
450 g (1 lb) cooked rice

For Sauce
2 tbs salted black beans
2 dried chillies
40 g (1½ oz) Ja Tsai Pickles
3 cloves garlic
2 tbs vegetable oil
300 ml (½ pint) good stock
1 chicken stock cube
2 tbs soya sauce
2–3 tbs tomato purée
3 tbs dry sherry
4 tbs cherry brandy

Preparation

Clean the crabs (they can be fresh or once boiled) and chop each shell into 2 pieces, and the body into 6 pieces (each piece with legs attached – the claws will need to be well-cracked). Clean and cut the leeks slantwise into 3.5 cm (1½ in) lengths. Finely chop the ginger. Finely chop the black beans, chillies, pickles and garlic. Heat the glutinous rice in 3 times its own volume of water. When it comes to the boil let it simmer gently for ½ hour.

Cooking

To prepare the sauce, heat the oil in a pan or wok. When hot, add the black beans, garlic, pickles and chillies. Stir-fry them for 1 min over a medium heat. Add the stock, crumble in the stock cube and add the soya sauce and tomato purée. Bring to the boil and simmer for 3 mins. Add sherry and brandy and turn the heat off.

Heat the oil in another wok. Stir-fry the ginger and leeks over a high heat for 4 mins. Sprinkle with salt and add the crab pieces. Stir and turn them with the leeks and ginger over a high heat for 3 mins. Pour in the sauce mixture. Bring to the boil, and turn the ingredients together in the sauce. Cover the wok, and cook for 5–6 mins.

Mix the cooked rice with the glutinous rice in a wok over a low heat. Reheat the crab sauce mixture and pour it over the mixed rice as a type of garnish. The sauce will seep through the rice, turning the latter into a highly delicious and substantial mass of food.

Stir-fried Bean Curd with Crab Meat and Black Bean Sauce *(for 4 people with rice and 1 vegetable dish)*

This is a very useful dish to cook when there are several mouths to feed and not much crab meat.

3 slices root-ginger
2 stalks spring onion
2–3 cakes bean curd
100 g (¼ lb) crab meat
4 tbs vegetable oil
75–100 g (3–4 oz) clams or mussels
1½ tbs cornflour (blended in 4 tbs cold water)

Sauce Ingredients
The same as for the previous recipe.

Preparation
Finely chop the ginger and the spring onions. Finely dice the bean curd. Finely flake the crab meat. Mix all the sauce ingredients in a bowl.

Cooking
Heat the oil in a wok and stir-fry the ginger and spring onions in it for ½ min. Add the clams and the crab meat and stir-fry over a medium heat for 1½ mins. Pour in the sauce. Bring to the boil and cook for 4–5 mins over a medium heat. Add the blended cornflour and stir. Finally, add the bean curd. Stir and turn the bean curd gently in the sauce with all the other ingredients. Simmer gently for 2 more mins.

Serving
Pour into a large bowl or tureen and serve from this. Ladle the dish into individual bowls of rice. The bean curd makes this a highly nutritious and flavoursome dish.

Braised Whole Fish in Black Bean Sauce *(for 4 people with 1 or 2 other dishes)*

1 whole fish (about 700–900 g/1½–2 lb) trout, sea bass, carp, perch, cod, etc.
salt and pepper (to taste)

- 2 tbs cornflour
- 2 rashers bacon
- 4 slices root-ginger
- 2 medium-sized onions
- 2 tbs salted black beans
- 50 g (2 oz) 'Snow Pickles' (or any pickles)
- 2 stalks spring onion
- 150 ml (¼ pint) good stock
- 2 tbs soya sauce
- 1 tbs chilli sauce
- 1 tbs wine vinegar
- 1 tbs cornflour (blended in 3 tbs cold water)
- 2 tbs sherry

Preparation

Clean and rub the fish with salt and pepper. Dredge with cornflour. Finely slice the bacon and ginger, cut the onion into very thin slices, coarsely chop the black beans and pickles. Finely chop the spring onions.

Cooking

Heat the oil in a wok. When a crumb will sizzle when dropped into it, lower the fish into the hot oil. Fry for 3 mins on both sides. Remove and drain. Pour all but 2 tbs of the oil away. Stir-fry the bacon, ginger, black beans and pickles in the hot oil for 1½ mins. Pour in the stock, bring to the boil and add the soya sauce, chilli sauce and vinegar. Stir and cook for 1½ mins. Lower the fish into the sauce and braise it over a medium heat for 7–8 mins, baste all the time. The sauce should reduce to a quarter of its original volume.

Transfer the fish on to a deep-sided oval dish. Add the blended cornflour and the sherry to the wok and stir in to the mixture. Cook for 1 min, stirring. Pour the sauce over the whole length of the fish on the serving dish.

Serving
Garnish the fish with the chopped spring onions. If fresh coriander leaves are available they may be used instead of spring onion or the two can be used together. This is a good dish to eat with rice. As it is a spicy and very rich dish it is best accompanied by a simple vegetable dish. You can double the quantity of fish used and 4 people could then easily manage it.

Dishes Using Oyster Sauce

Although oysters are used and eaten extensively all along the East Coast of China south of the Yangtze River, oyster sauce is used as a normal flavouring ingredient only in the provinces of Kwangtung and Fukien, where it is frequently added to dishes to make them more savoury. It is then applied to meats, vegetables and noodles and seems to add a new dimension to them.

Beef in Oyster Sauce (for 4 people with 1 or 2 other dishes)

  450 g (1 lb) beef steak (fillet, rump, topside, sirloin, etc.)
  1½ tsp salt
  pepper (to taste)
  1½ tbs cornflour
  ½ egg white
  2 slices root-ginger
  1 green pepper
  4 tbs vegetable oil
  4 tbs good stock
  2 tbs oyster sauce
  1½ tbs dry sherry
  1½ tbs soya sauce

Preparation
Cut the beef into very thin slices 6 × 5 cm (2½ × 2 in). Sprinkle and rub with salt and pepper, dredge with cornflour, and wet with egg white. Finely chop the ginger and cut the pepper into 2.5 × 7 cm (1 × 3 in) strips.

Cooking
Heat the oil in a wok. Stir-fry the ginger in the oil for ½ min. Add the beef slices and stir-fry in the hot oil for 1¼ mins. Remove with a slotted spoon and set aside. Add the green pepper and stir-fry for 1 min. Add the stock, oyster sauce, sherry and soya sauce. Stir over a high heat for ¼ min. Return the beef slices to the wok, and stir and turn them in the sauce for 1 min.

Serving
This is a very appealing dish for those who like highly savoury foods. It is excellent eaten with plain rice and a simple vegetable dish.

Cantonese Ham and Onion Omelette with Oyster Sauce
(for 4 people with 1 or 2 other dishes)

   5 eggs
   1 tsp salt
   pepper (to taste)
   2 medium-sized onions
   75–100 g (3–4 oz) ham
   3 stalks spring onion
   2 cloves garlic
   4 tbs vegetable oil
   1½ tbs lard
   1½ tbs soya sauce
   2 tbs good stock
   2½ tbs oyster sauce
   2 tbs dry sherry

Preparation
Crack the eggs into a bowl, add the salt and pepper and beat lightly. Cut the onions into very thin slices and the ham into thin matchsticks. Finely chop the spring onions. Coarsely chop the garlic.

Cooking
Heat the oil in a wok. Lift the handle of the wok so that a larger area of the surface of the wok is evenly greased. Add the onion, and stir-fry in the hot oil for ½ min. Add the ham and stir-fry for 1 min. Pour in the eggs. After ¼ min stir the egg with the onion and ham. Allow the mixture to cook undisturbed for ½ min by which time most of the egg will have set. Remove and transfer to a well-heated serving dish. Add the lard, garlic and spring onions to the wok. Stir them around a few times. Add the soya sauce, stock, oyster sauce and sherry. Bring to the boil, stirring a few times.

Serving
Pour the sauce evenly over the stir-fried omelette in the serving dish. This is a very satisfying dish which should be eaten with rice and a vegetable or meat dish or both.

Stir-Fried Bean Curd in Oyster Sauce *(for 4 people with 1 or 2 other dishes)*

6 medium Chinese dried mushrooms
100 g (¼ lb) firm button mushrooms
3 cakes bean curd
3 tbs vegetable oil
1½ tbs lard
100 g (¼ lb) minced pork or beef
1 tsp salt
4 tbs peas
4 tbs good stock

3 tbs soya sauce
1 tbs hoisin sauce
3 tbs oyster sauce
1 tbs chilli sauce
1 tbs cornflour (blended in 3 tbs cold water)

Preparation

Soak the dried mushrooms in hot water for 20 mins. Drain. Discard the stems and cut each cap into quarters. Wash and cut the button mushrooms into thin slices. Cut the bean curd into 18–24 small cubes.

Cooking

Heat the oil and lard in a wok. When it is hot add the minced meat, pepper and salt and stir-fry over a medium heat for 1 min. Add dried mushrooms and stir-fry them with the beef for 1 min. Add the mushrooms and continue stir-frying for another min. Add the peas, stock, soya, hoisin, oyster and chilli sauce. Cook, turning the mixture until it boils and bubbles. Stir in the blended cornflour. Add the bean curd cubes and turn them in the sauce until they are well coated and cooked through. Simmer for 5 mins by which time they should have taken on the flavour of the sauce.

Serving

Serve in a large bowl or deep-sided serving dish. This makes a substantial quantity of highly nutritious foods. It is easily digested by the aged, inexpensive to produce, and recognized as a family dish which can be served to any diner.

Broccoli in Crab Meat and Oyster Sauce *(for 4 people with 1 or 2 other dishes including 1 meat dish)*

800 g (1¾ lb) broccoli
125 ml (¼ pint) vegetable oil

2½ tbs oyster sauce
2½ tbs good stock
1½ tbs soya sauce
1 tsp salt
pepper (to taste)

For Crab Sauce
100–125 g (4–5 oz) cooked crab meat
2 slices root-ginger
2 stalks spring onion
1½ tbs lard
1 tbs light soya sauce
2 tbs dry sherry
4 tbs good stock
1 tbs cornflour (blended in 3 tbs cold water)

Preparation
Wash and break the broccoli into individual florets. Cut the stems slantwise into 2.5–3.5 cm (1–1½ in) slices. Flake the crab meat, cut the ginger and spring onions finely.

Cooking
Heat the oil in a wok. When it is hot add the broccoli and turn in the hot oil with a slotted spoon for 3 mins. Be careful not to burn it. Drain away all the oil (reserve for other uses). Sprinkle the broccoli with oyster sauce, soya sauce and stock. Season to taste with salt and pepper. Stir and turn in the wok for a further 1 min and transfer to a serving dish.

Heat the lard in a wok. Add the ginger, spring onions, and crab meat. Stir over a medium heat for 1 min. Add the soya sauce, sherry and stock. When it starts to boil, stir in the blended cornflour. Turn and stir a few times. Spoon on top of the broccoli in the serving dish.

Serving
The crab meat sauce enhances the appeal of this simple vegetable dish and makes it fit for serving at a banquet, which is where it is often seen nowadays.

Index

Asparagus
  'Boil-in-the-Water' Asparagus with Bean Sprouts, 153
  Braised Duck with Asparagus, Bamboo Shoots and Mushrooms, 104
  Pork, Mushroom, Marrow and Asparagus Soup, 78

Aubergine
  Braised Aubergine with Bean Curd Cheese, 126
  Steamed Aubergine with Tomatoes and Dried Shrimps, 55
  'Yu Hsiang' Aubergine, 143

Bamboo Shoots, 68
  Braised Duck, with Asparagus, Bamboo Shoots and Mushrooms, 104
  Stir-fried Bean Sprouts and Bamboo Shoots with Shredded Pork, 119

Bean Curd, 67
  Braised Aubergine with Bean Curd Cheese, 126
  Crab Meat, Bean Curd and Lotus Seed Soup, 76
  Fish Head and Bean Curd Main Course Soup, 73
  Ma-Po Tou-Fu, 163
  Plain Boiled Bean Curd with Hot Dressing, 162
  Spinach and Bean Curd Soup with Shredded Ham, 74
  Stir-fried Bean Curd with Crab Meat and Black Bean Sauce, 194
  Stir-fried and Braised Bean Curd with Minced Meat and Chinese Dried Mushrooms, 138
  Stir-fried Bean Curd in Oyster Sauce, 199
  Stir-fried Courgettes with Peas, Tomatoes and Mashed Bean Curd, 128

Bean Paste Sauce, 39, 40, 145

Bean Sprouts
  Quick-fried Chicken Slices with Bean Sprouts and Red Peppers, 97
  Stir-fried Bean Sprouts and Bamboo Shoots with Shredded Pork, 119
  Stir-fried Bean Sprouts with Shredded Pork, 53

Beef
  Beef in Oyster Sauce, 197
  Quick-fried Beef Ribbons with Sliced Onions, 48
  Sliced Beef and Tomato Soup, 33
  Smoked Beef, 157
  Stir-fried Beef in Black Bean Sauce with Noodles, 190
  Szechuan Sliced Beef in 'Ma-La' Sauce, 152
  West Lake Minced Beef Soup with Watercress, 176

Black Bean Sauce, 188
  Braised Whole Fish in Black Bean Sauce, 195
  Fukien Crab Rice with Leeks and Black Bean Sauce, 193
  Quick-fried Chicken in Black Bean Sauce, 189
  Quick-fried Scallops and Prawns with Black Bean Sauce, 191
  Stir-fried Bean Curd with Crab Meat and Black Bean Sauce, 194
  Stir-fried Sliced Beef in Black Bean Sauce with Noodles, 190

Boil-in-the-Water, 153

Braising, 16

Index

Broccoli
  Broccoli in Crab Meat and Oyster Sauce, 200
  Duck-and-Chicken Rice with Broccoli and Spring Cabbage, 103
  Quick-fried Marinated Breast of Chicken with Broccoli, 99
Buddhist 'Food of the Forest for the Immortals', 58

Cauliflower Fu-Yung, 123
Celery
  Braised Celery with Two Types of Mushrooms, 127
Cha Siu Barbecued and Roast Meats, 179
Chicken
  Bang Bang Chicken, 151
  Chicken and Sweetcorn Soup with Crab Meat, 169
  Crispy and Spicy Chicken Liver and Gizzards, 187
  Deep-fried Crispy Chicken, 186
  Drunken Chicken, 96
  Duck-and-Chicken Rice with Broccoli and Spring Cabbage, 103
  Gold and Silver or Chicken and Duck Congee, 178
  Lotus Leaf Wrapped Long Steamed Chicken, 148
  Minced Chicken Soup with Croûtons and Ham, 37
  Quick-fried Chicken in Black Bean Sauce, 189
  Quick-fried Chicken Cubes with Master Sauce, Cooked Kidney and Liver on Crispy Noodles, 100
  Quick-fried Chicken Slices with Bean Sprouts and Red Peppers, 97
  Quick-fried Diced Chicken Cubes in Yellow Bean Paste Sauce, 39
  Quick-fried Diced Chicken with Gammon and Cucumber Cubes, 39
  Quick-fried Marinated Breast of Chicken with Broccoli, 99
  Quick-fried Shredded Chicken with French Beans, 52
  Shanghai Quick-Braised Chicken on the Bone, 95
  Sliced Chicken and Abalone Soup with Chinese Dried Mushrooms, 168
  Smoked Chicken, 157
  Steamed Ground-Rice Lotus-Leaf Wrapped Chicken in Onion Oil, 101
  Yangchow Main Course Chicken Soup, 71
Chinese Cabbage, 26
  'Boil-in-the-Water' Chinese Cabbage with Shredded Ham, 154
  Duck Liver and Chinese White Cabbage Soup, 36
  Red-cooked Chinese Cabbage, 51
  Sliced Duck Liver Soup with Chinese Cabbage, 34
  'White-braised' Chinese Cabbage with Shrimps, 50
Chow Mien, 61
  Shrimp Chow Mien, 92
Congee, 84, 177
  Chicken and Duck Congee, 178
  Fish and Seafood Congee, 179
Coriander, 25
Courgettes
  Stir-fried Courgettes with Peas, Tomatoes and Mashed Bean Curd, 128
Crab
  Broccoli in Crab Meat and Oyster Sauce, 200
  Chicken and Sweetcorn Soup with Crab Meat, 169
  Chingkiang Pork and Crab Meat Lion's Head Meatballs, 118
  Crab Meat, Bean Curd and Lotus Seed Soup, 76
  Crab Meat and Lettuce Leaf Soup, 171
  Fukien Crab Rice with Leeks and Black Bean Sauce, 193
  Savoury Steamed Egg-Custard with Crab Meat, 56

Index

Stir-fried Bean Curd with Crab
  Meat and Black Bean Sauce,
  194

Deep frying, 20
Doong Chai, 18
Duck
  Aromatic and Crispy Duck,
    156
  Braised Duck with Asparagus,
    Bamboo Shoots and
    Mushrooms, 104
  Chicken and Duck Congee,
    178
  Duck-and-Chicken Rice with
    Broccoli and Spring Cabbage,
    103
  Duck Liver and Chinese White
    Cabbage Soup, 36
  Hangchow Duck cooked in
    Master Sauce, 105
  Sliced Duck Liver Soup with
    Chinese Cabbage, 34
  Smoked Duck, 157
  The Soochow Red Soya Duck,
    107

Eggs
  Ham and Egg Fried Rice, 81
  Savoury Steamed Egg-custard
    with Crab Meat, 56
  Stir-fried Eggs with Onion and
    Tomatoes, 57

Fish
  Braised Whole Fish in Black
    Bean Sauce, 195
  Braised Whole Fish in Hot
    Vinegar Sauce, 109
  Braised Whole Fish with Salted
    Pickles, 108
  Chingkiang Riverside Noodles,
    88
  Fish and Clam Soup with
    Oysters (or Mussels), 170
  Fish and Dried Shrimp Soft
    Rice, 84
  Fish Head and Bean Curd Main
    Course Soup, 73
  Fish Fu-Yung, 116
  Fish and Seafood Congee, 179
  Fishball Soup with Watercress,
    172
  Fried Rice with Fresh Fish and
    Salt Fish, 83
  Garnished Steamed Fillet of
    Fish, 113
  Minced or Flaked Fish Soup
    with Ham and Croûtons, 39
  Poached Fishballs with Shrimps
    and Mushrooms, 114
  Shallow-fried Onion-smothered
    Fish, 49
  Sliced Fish Pepperpot Soup, 31
  Sliced Fillet of Fish in Yu
    Hsiang Combination, 141
  Squirrel Fish, 111
  Sweet and Sour Fish Steaks,
    182
  Szechuan 'Tou-Pan' Fish
    Steaks, 145
  Whole Fish Soup, 75
  Yangtze Fish Salad, 115
  See Also Crab, Prawns, Shrimps
French Beans
  Quick-fried French Beans with
    Dried Shrimps, 125
Frogs' Legs
  Leek and Frogs' Legs Soup, 175
Fukien Crab Rice with Leeks and
  Black Bean Sauce, 193

Ham
  'Boil-in-the-Water' Chinese
    Cabbage with Shredded
    Ham, 154
  Cantonese Ham and Onion
    Omelette with Oyster Sauce,
    198
  Ham and Egg Fried Rice, 81
  Minced Chicken Soup with
    Croûtons and Ham, 37
  Minced or Flaked Fish Soup
    with Ham and Croûtons, 39
  Quick-fried Diced Chicken with
    Gammon and Cucumber
    Cubes, 39
  Quick-fried Diced Ham with
    Shrimps and Lotus Seeds, 121
  Spinach and Bean Curd Soup
    with Shredded Ham, 74
Hoisin sauce, 19
Hseuh Chai, 18

Index

Ja Tsai Pickles, 18, 158
   Noodle Soup with Shredded Pork and Ja Tsai Pickles, 159
   Quick-fried Shredded Pork with Ja Tsai Pickles and Bean Sprouts, 158

Lamb
   Mongolian Hot Pot, 27
   Sliced Lamb Pepperpot Soup with Sliced Cucumber, 32

Leeks
   Fukien Crab Rice with Leeks and Black Bean Sauce, 193
   Leek and Frogs' Legs Soup, 175

Lotus Leaf Wrapped Ground Rice Pork, 150

Lotus Leaf Wrapped Long Steamed Chicken, 148

Lotus Seeds
   Crab Meat, Bean Curd and Lotus Seed Soup, 76
   Quick-fried Diced Ham with Shrimps and Lotus Seeds, 121

Ma-La, 151

Marrow
   Pork, Mushroom, Marrow and Asparagus Soup, 78

Ma-Po Tou-Fu, 163

Master Sauce, 154

Meat *see* Beef, Chicken, etc.

Mixed Vegetables with Pea-starch Transparent Noodles, 124

Mongolian Hot Pot, 27

Mushrooms
   Braised Celery with Two Types of Mushrooms, 127
   Braised Duck with Asparagus, Bamboo Shoots and Mushrooms, 104
   Poached Fishballs, with Shrimps and Mushrooms, 114
   Pork, Mushroom, Marrow and Asparagus Soup, 78
   Sliced Chicken and Abalone Soup with Chinese Dried Mushrooms, 168

Noodles, 28–9
   Chingkiang Riverside Noodles, 88
   Dan Dan Noodles, 161
   Mixed Vegetables with Pea-Starch Transparent Noodles, 124
   Noodle Soup with Shredded Pork and Ja Tsai Pickles, 159
   Peking Boiled Noodles in Minced Meat Sauce, 60
   Pickle and Shredded Pork Noodles, 94
   Quick-fried Noodles with Shredded Meat and Vegetables, 61
   Shanghai Cold-Tossed Noodles, 87
   Shrimp Chow Mien, 92
   Three Shrimp Cooked Noodles, 90
   Three Shrimp Noodles, 92
   Transparent Noodles, 44
   Vegetarian Cooked-in-the-Wok Noodles, 59
   'Yu Hsiang' Vegetables with Transparent Pea-Starch Noodles, 142

Oyster Sauce, 197
   Beef in Oyster Sauce, 197
   Broccoli in Crab Meat and Oyster Sauce, 200
   Cantonese Ham and Onion Omelette with Oyster Sauce, 198
   Stir-fried Bean Curd in Oyster Sauce, 199

Pasta, 28

Pickles, 18
   Pickle and Shredded Pork Noodles, 94
   See Also Snow Pickles

Pork
   Chingkiang Pork and Crab Meat Lion's Head Meatballs, 118
   Crispy Skinned Pork, 185
   Double-Cooked Pork, 136
   Lotus Leaf Wrapped Ground Rice Pork, 150
   Marinated Barbecued Pork, 180
   Pickle and Shredded Pork Noodles, 94

Index

Pork, Mushroom, Marrow and Asparagus Soup, 78
Pork Spare-rib and Cucumber Soup, 79
'Proletarian' Yellow Bean and Shredded Pork Soup, 77
Quick-fried Five Shredded Ingredients, 43
Quick-fried Shredded Pork with Ja Tsai Pickles and Bean Sprouts, 158
Quick-fried Shredded Pork with 'Yu Hsiang' Combination of Shredded Ingredients, 139
Quick-fried Three Types of Diced Meat Cubes in Bean Paste Sauce, 40
Sliced Pork in 'Tou-Pan' Sauce with Green Peppers, 147
Stir-fried Bean Sprouts and Bamboo Shoots with Shredded Pork, 119
Stir-fried Bean Sprouts with Shredded Pork, 53
Stir-fried and Braised Chinese Spare-ribs, 47
Stir-fried Pork, Dried Shrimps and Vegetables with Pea-Starch Transparent Noodles, 44
Stir-fried Shredded Pork with Leeks and Transparent Noodles, 44
Sweet and Sour Pork, 181
Sweet and Sour Pork Chops, 120
Szechuan Dry-Fried Pork-Cubes, Quick-fried Chillies and Peppercorns, 137
White-cooked Sliced Pork, 46

Prawns
Quick-fried Prawns in 'Tou-Pan' Sauce, 146
Quick-fried Scallops and Prawns with Black Bean Sauce, 191
Sweet and Sour Prawns, 183

Red oil, 135
Rice
Congee, 84, 177
Fish and Dried Shrimp Soft Rice, 84
Fried Rice with Fresh Fish and Salt Fish, 83
Ham and Egg Fried Rice, 81
Vegetarian Fried Rice, 85
Yangchow Fried Rice, 80

Scallops
Quick-fried Scallops and Prawns with Black Bean Sauce, 191

Shrimps
Fish and Dried Shrimp Soft Rice, 84
Poached Fishballs with Shrimps and Mushrooms, 114
Quick-fried Diced Ham with Shrimps and Lotus Seeds, 121
Quick-fried French Beans with Dried Shrimps, 125
Shrimp Chow Mien, 92
Steamed Aubergines with Tomatoes and Dried Shrimps, 55
Stir-fried Pork, Dried Shrimps and Vegetables with Pea-Starch Transparent Noodles, 44
Stir-fried Spinach with Garlic and Dried Shrimps, 54
Three Shrimp Cooked Noodles, 90
Three Shrimp Noodles, 92
'White-braised' Chinese Cabbage with Shrimps, 50

Snow Pickles, 18, 67, 94, 108, 119

Soups
Chicken and Sweetcorn Soup with Crab Meat, 169
Crab Meat, Bean Curd and Lotus Seed Soup, 76
Crab Meat and Lettuce Leaf Soup, 171
Duck Liver and Chinese White Cabbage Soup, 36
Fish and Clam Soup with Oysters (or Mussels), 170
Fishball Soup with Watercress, 172
Fish Head and Bean Curd Main Course Soup, 73

Four-Colour Soup, 72
Hot and Sour Soup, 30, 160
Leek and Frogs' Legs Soup, 175
Minced Chicken Soup with Croûtons and Ham, 37
Minced or Flaked Fish Soup with Ham and Croûtons, 39
Noodle Soup with Shredded Pork and Ja Tsai Pickle, 159
Pork, Mushroom, Marrow and Asparagus Soup, 78
Pork Spare-rib and Cucumber Soup, 79
'Proletarian' Yellow Bean and Shredded Pork Soup, 77
Sliced Beef and Tomato Soup, 33
Sliced Chicken and Abalone Soup with Chinese Dried Mushrooms, 168
Sliced Duck Liver Soup with Chinese Cabbage, 34
Sliced Fish Pepperpot Soup, 31
Sliced Lamb Pepperpot Soup with Sliced Cucumber, 32
Spinach and Bean Curd Soup with Shredded Ham, 74
Three Chopped and Three Shredded Ingredients Soup, 70
West Lake Minced Beef Soup with Watercress, 176
Whole Fish Soup, 75
Wontun Soup, 174
Yangchow Main Course Chicken Soup, 71
Soya Paste, 19, 25
Soya Sauce, 19
Spare-ribs
Stir-fried and Braised Chinese Spare-ribs, 47
Pork Spare-rib and Cucumber Soup, 79

Spinach
Spinach and Bean Curd Soup with Shredded Ham, 74
Stir-fried Spinach with Garlic and Dried Shrimps, 54
Spring Cabbage
Duck-and-Chicken Rice with Broccoli and Spring Cabbage, 103
Spring Rolls, 27
Squirrel Fish, 111
Steaming, 20
Stewing, 16
Stir-frying, 14–16
Sweet and Sour Fish Steaks, 182
Sweet and Sour Pork, 181
Sweet and Sour Prawns, 183
Sweet and Sour Sauce, 26
Szechuan Hot Pickle, 18
Szechuan 'Tou-Pan' Fish Steaks, 145

Tomatoes
Sliced Beef and Tomato Soup, 33
Steamed Aubergine with Tomatoes and Dried Shrimps, 55
Stir-fried Courgettes with Peas, Tomatoes and Mashed Bean Curd, 128
'Tou-Pan' Bean Paste Sauce, 145

Winter Pickle, 18

Yellow Beans
'Proletarian' Yellow Bean and Shredded Pork Soup, 77
Yu Hsiang, 139–40
Yu Hsiang Aubergine, 143
Yu Hsiang Vegetables with Transparent Pea-Starch Noodles, 142